# LET'S MAKE CANDY

# LET'S MAKE CANDY

BY NOY ALEXANDER

EDITED BY JANET WERNER

CHARLES E. TUTTLE CO.: PUBLISHERS
RUTLAND, VERMONT & TOKYO, JAPAN

*Representatives*
*Continental Europe:* BOXERBOOKS, INC., *Zurich*
*British Isles:* PRENTICE-HALL INTERNATIONAL, INC., *London*
*Australasia:* PAUL FLESCH & CO., PTY. LTD., *Melbourne*
*Canada:* M. G. HURTIG LTD., *Edmonton*

*Published by Charles E. Tuttle Co., Inc.*
*of Rutland, Vermont & Tokyo, Japan*
*with editorial offices at*
*Suido 1-chome, 2-6, Bunkyo-ku, Tokyo*

*Library of Congress*
*Catalog Card No. 65–19806*

*International Standard Book No. 0-8048-0361-7*

*First edition, 1965*
*Fourth printing, 1971*

*Book design & typography*
*by Keiko Chiba*
*Printed in Japan*

# TABLE OF CONTENTS

# INTRODUCTION

What suits your fancy? Shall it be rich chocolate fudge? Smooth vanilla creams? Light fluffy divinity? Flavorful molasses taffy? Chewy caramels? Or do you want to try your hand at dipping chocolates? Whatever it is that suits your fancy, whether you want a small quantity for family and friends or a large quantity for a profitable business or charity function, you'll find candy making easy and fun—and the results delicious.

The nutritive value of candy is high and in a concentrated form. Its ingredients such as nutmeats, peanut butter, milk chocolate, and all milk products add protein to the diet and, like other sweets, candy is high in the carbohydrates which the body needs for energy.

Candy, because it keeps well, is always ready to serve for a snack or a finish for a meal. Since homemade candy is inexpensive, such things as assorted chocolates, candied fruits, coarsely ground crunches and brittles used for toppings, fresh strawberries with center mounds of crushed mints, and stuffed fruits often provide the ideal solution to the perennial problem of what to serve for dessert.

1. Assorted candy

# EQUIPMENT FOR CANDY MAKING

Many candies can be made with elementary kitchen equipment. Let's look at the simple utensils needed.

SAUCEPANS (average sizes from 1 to 6 quarts): A medium-weight aluminum pan may be used for most candy, but a *heavy* metal pan (aluminum or iron) is essential for the candies cooked to a higher temperature. The heavier metal pans hold a more uniform heat, and the candy does not stick so readily or scorch while cooking.

MEASURING CUPS and SPOONS

WOODEN SPOONS

KNIVES, SPATULAS, and SCISSORS

SHALLOW PANS and COOKIE SHEETS

TRAYS, COOKIE SHEETS, or LIGHT-WEIGHT BOARDS: Used to hold chocolate-dipped candy.

TINS and HEAVY PAPER BOXES: Used as containers for storing candy.

LARGE HEAVY PLATTER: Useful for cooling and creaming candy without a marble slab.

ELECTRIC BEATER

DOUBLE BOILER

WOODEN CUTTING BOARD

WIRE STRAINER

WAX PAPER, ALUMINUM FOIL, PLASTIC WRAP, and PLASTIC BAGS

DEEP PIE or CAKE TIN, SHALLOW SAUCEPAN, or SMALL LIGHT-WEIGHT SKILLET (about 8″ or 9″ in diameter): Used to hold chocolate for dipping.

Packing Boxes and Paper Candy Cups: Used to package candy. Available from paper manufacturing companies.

In addition, there are three important pieces of equipment you should have to make candy making easier.

Candy Thermometer: Used to accurately test temperature of candy sirup.

Marble Slab: Used to cool and cream candies quickly. A $24'' \times 36''$ size is convenient for all home candy making. It is large enough, without the use of steel bars, to cool candies for creaming if there is up to 8 cups of sugar in the recipe. A marble piece $18'' \times 24''$ is large enough for a batch of candy using up to 4 cups of sugar. Sold by confectioner supply houses or can be made by marble companies. Any clean piece of marble, such as an old dresser or table top, may be used.

Candy Spatulas (2 spatulas): Used for creaming candy more easily. These are putty or paint scrapers with $3''$–$5''$ stiff blades. Found in hardware or paint supply houses.

You may want to add this equipment when you delve further into the art of candy making.

Steel Bars: Useful but not essential, except when making candy in large quantities. Steel bars that form walls on four sides of the marble slab are used to keep large quantities of candy from running off the slab. They also regulate the candy's size and thickness. Bars are $\frac{3}{4}''$ wide and $12''$ long, or longer if desired. Four bars are used. Sold by confectioner supply houses or can be made by bar metal companies.

Dipping Forks: Used for fondant or chocolate dipping. Use dinner forks or fondant dippers which are sold at confectioner supply houses.

Funnel and Stick: Used in making mint patties with melted fondant. Sold in confectioner supply houses.

TAFFY HOOK: Useful when pulling large amount of taffy. Sold in confectioner supply houses.

KITCHEN SCALES: Used to more accurately measure ingredients used in candy recipes.

MEDICINE DROPPER: Used to more accurately measure small amounts of oil flavoring and acids.

## CANDY INGREDIENTS

Do you think candies are made of unusual or hard-to-get or expensive ingredients? Check the following list of major candy ingredients. You'll see most of them on the shelves of your grocery store. To insure good candy, be sure the ingredients are of high quality and fresh.

SUGARS: Main ingredient in candies.
1. Granulated
2. Confectioners' or powdered
3. Light or dark brown: Light brown sugar is more desirable for most candy.

SIRUPS: Used in candy making to retard or prevent graining, to give body and flavor, and to help keep creamed candies soft.
1. Corn sirup: Easiest and most effective ingredient used to control graining. Gives a slightly heavier texture than acids, thus the candy will have more body.
2. Molasses
3. Maple sirup
4. Honey
5. Sorghum

ACIDS (harmless organic acids): Help prevent formation of noticeable-sized sugar crystals.
1. Cream of tartar
2. Acetic acid (36%): Obtained in drug stores.
3. Vinegar
4. Lemon juice and other fruit acids

Note: Since vinegar, lemon juice, and other fruit juices vary in their acid content, cream of tartar and acetic acid are more dependable. Cream of tartar is most satisfactory because it is uniform in its acid content and is inexpensive. Since acids are erratic in their action, they should be measured accurately.

DAIRY PRODUCTS
1. Cream
2. Butter
3. Milk: Fresh, non-fat dry, evaporated, and condensed.

COLORINGS
1. Pastes, powders, or liquid: Liquid coloring is easiest to blend into creamed candy mixtures.

FLAVORINGS
1. Extracts
2. Oils: Much stronger than extracts. Measure carefully. Obtained in drug stores.

EGGS

UNFLAVORED GELATIN

GLYCERIN: Used to help keep candy soft. Buy a pure glycerin in drug stores.

NUTMEATS

FRUIT: Fresh, frozen, and dried.

VEGETABLE FATS: Margarine, other solid fats, and oils.

CHOCOLATE
1. Unsweetened (also called baking and liquor)
2. Dark sweet (also called semi-sweet)
3. Bittersweet
4. Milk chocolate

COCOA

WATER: Pure, clean tap water (strongly flavored waters may affect the flavor of candy).

CORNSTARCH

# GENERAL INFORMATION FOR CANDY MAKING

You have good ingredients, and you have the basic equipment necessary. Now take a minute to read some helpful hints on what to do if candy making is to be easy, fun, and successful.

Read carefully through the entire recipe. Assemble all the ingredients and equipment needed.

Measure the ingredients in the recipe into the proper-size pan. To prevent boil-overs, allow about a 1-quart space for each cup of sugar used.

Mix ingredients thoroughly before placing the pan over the heat.

When using flavoring, it's fairly safe to use 1 teaspoon of flavoring extract for 2 cups of sugar in a candy recipe. Flavoring oils are very strong, so it's better to add only 2 or 3 drops and then taste. "Flavor to taste" is a good rule.

Stir all candy mixtures (unless otherwise stated) at the beginning of cooking over moderate heat until the sugar is dissolved and boiling starts. This prevents sugar crystals from sticking together or adhering to the pan which might cause the candy to grain. Stir slowly and carefully to avoid leaving sugar crystals made by splashing on the sides of the pan.

Cover all sugar and water mixtures for the first 2 or 3 minutes of boiling. This softens the sugar crystals which form on the sides of the pan. Uncover the pan and keep the crystals wiped down with a cloth wrapped around the tines of a fork and dipped in hot water (or use a pastry brush or clean sponge).

Do not cover candy mixtures using milk products or molasses while cooking. Because they foam, if the steam cannot escape, they may boil over.

Boil sugar and water mixtures quickly. Cook cream or

milk mixtures less rapidly, but briskly. As the sirup gets thicker, cook more slowly.

Remove the pan from the heat immediately when the final test is reached to insure not overcooking.

For candies cooked at higher temperatures, the last few degrees must be reached by very slow cooking because the thermometer goes up rapidly.

Do not scrape the hot candy from the pan when pouring, but let it drip out. Scraping may cause the candy to grain.

In a heavy pan, the temperature of the candy sirup may climb several degrees after the pan has been removed from the heat. If the candy is to stand in the pan, cool the pan quickly by setting it in cold water for a few seconds.

On very warm humid days, cook candy 1 or 2 degrees higher because it is more likely to absorb moisture from the air while it is cooling.

When candy is mistakenly cooked past the temperature desired, add a little water and recook to the proper degree.

Marble slabs should be dampened or greased before they are used. Dampen with a cold damp cloth or grease with butter, margarine, or oil.

When marble slabs are used to cool candy for creaming, allow several hours for the slabs to cool before using them again. To cool marble quickly, cover it with ice cubes.

Unless otherwise stated in the recipe, you need not stir or beat candy vigorously at any time. Stir only enough to keep the mixture in motion.

STORING CANDY

Do not pack or store different types of candy together. The hard-cooked candy will absorb moisture from the air or from the softer cooked candy and may get sticky. If, however, hard-cooked candies are securely wrapped or coated with chocolate, they may be packed with other candy types.

Store all candy tightly covered in a cool place at about 65°F.

## Freezing Candy

To keep any candy fresh, it may be frozen, but creamed candy and chocolate-coated candy may be frozen most successfully. Wrap the candy securely in moisture-proof paper or put it in plastic bags which must be sealed tightly before the candy is put in the freezer.

2. Wrapping fudge for freezing

When removing candy from the freezer, let it stand for 6 to 8 hours to warm to room temperature before opening or removing the wrapping. This prevents moisture from collecting on the candy from the temperature change.

Coated candy which is already boxed and ready for gift giving may be frozen. Put the boxes in plastic bags and seal tightly before freezing.

CANDY THERMOMETER

Test the candy thermometer for accuracy by putting it in a pan of cold water with the mercury bulb completely submerged. Bring the water to a boil and let it continue to boil for several minutes. This determines the temperature at which water boils in your locality. The thermometer should register 212°F at or near sea level on a day with standard atmospheric pressure. If the temperature registers above 212°F, add that number of degrees to the temperature given in the recipe. If the temperature registers below 212°F, subtract that number of degrees.

To use the thermometer, have it warm when you insert it in the hot sirup and lower it gradually. Put the thermometer in the candy mixture after the sugar is dissolved and the mixture starts to boil. When you are finished with the thermometer, remove it from the hot sirup and put it in a pan of hot water.

To read the thermometer, hold it in an upright position with the mercury bulb completely submerged in the boiling sirup. Your eye should be level with the top of the mercury.

TEMPERATURE TESTS

A candy thermometer is the only accurate way to measure temperature—a most important part of candy making. Results cannot be depended upon without a thermometer.

If, however, you do not have a thermometer, make a cold water test for candy by dropping a small amount of the candy mixture into cold water. Use fresh cold water each time. To insure not overcooking, remove the pan from the heat while making the cold water test, especially nearing the final test.

COLD WATER TEMPERATURE TESTS

Soft Ball: 234°F–240°F
   Forms a soft ball which can be picked up, but which flattens on standing.
Firm Ball: 242°F–248°F
   Forms a firm ball and holds its shape.

Hard Ball: 250°F–265°F
   Forms a very hard ball which holds its shape.
Soft Crack: 270°F–285°F
   Separates into threads in cold water. Threads will make
   a cracking sound when hit against the side of a cup.
Hard Crack: 295°F–310°F
   Separates into heavy threads in cold water. Threads
   are hard and brittle.

## CANDY MAKING WHYS AND WHEREFORES

Perhaps after reading the general information on candy
making, you have many questions in your mind. If candy is
so simple to make, if the ingredients are such common ones,
why must some rules and regulations be so rigidly followed?
For those who like some technical information to supplement
their practical knowledge, let's delve a bit into the whys
and wherefores of sugar cookery.

Sugar is the main ingredient in candy. The basic tech-
nique in candy making is to control the behavior of the
grains (crystals) of sugar which are dissolved by liquids and
heat. There are two basic classifications of candy: grained
and ungrained. The grained candies include all creams,
fondants, and fudges; the ungrained include caramels, nougat, brittles, and hard candies.

All creamed candies are known as grained candies. Small
grains are necessary and act as seeds to start the creaming
process when the working (creaming or beating) is begun.
In a smooth-textured creamed candy, these grains are kept
small and unnoticeable by four things: 1) the right amount
of interfering agent 2) proper cooking 3) proper cooling 4)
proper working of the candy. Too little sirup or acid may
produce excessive graining of creamed candies, and on the
other hand, too much sirup or acid will keep the mixture too
liquid and make the candy too soft to cream. The use of fat,

milk solids, egg, and air in beating further aids in coating the small sugar crystals to give a smooth creamy texture.

When a large quantity of sirup and acid is used in proportion to the amount of sugar, we get an ungrained candy. Even with stirring and scraping during the cooking process, these candies should not grain much, if at all. Certain ingredients, such as sirups and acids, are known as interfering agents. The sirup may be corn sirup, molasses, or honey, and acids are cream of tartar, vinegar, and fruit juice. These interfering agents aid in liquifying the sugar grains and preventing them from re-forming into noticeable-sized grains when proper methods of cooking and cooling are used.

# CREAMED CANDY

Creamed candies depend on few ingredients and the careful following of cooking instructions for successful results. Included in this largest group of candy are such favorites as vanilla creams, fudge, butter fondant, and orientals. The characteristic fine texture and velvety smoothness of creamed candy is a result of the air that is introduced when the cooled sirup is worked.

Variations are a-plenty in this section, so you'll find that a few basic recipes soon open up a whole world of candies! Because the methods of making all creamed candies are similar, you will want to read some general information before you start.

Coffee or all-purpose cream (18% butterfat) makes a good creamed candy. For richer candy, heavier cream may be substituted. Fresh whole milk or evaporated milk diluted to milk consistency may be used if you add 2 tablespoons of butter or margarine for each cup of milk used. Milk mixtures require some stirring during cooking to prevent sticking and scorching.

Most candy should be cooled to lukewarm (110°F) or

cooler before you start to work it. With the back of your hand, test the temperature of the candy in the center of the batch—the edges cool more quickly.

Since candy for creaming should be cooled quickly, a marble slab is desirable, but candy may be cooled on a platter or pan which has been placed on a wire rack to allow air to get underneath. It may take only a few minutes to cool small amounts of candy on a cold marble slab.

To "work" (also termed "cream" or "beat") candy, stir it with candy spatulas on a slab or with wooden spoons in a pan or on a platter. To work the candy, hold one spatula in each hand, start at the bottom (the side closest to you), and scrape the candy mixture up around the sides and back down through the center. Keep working the mixture until the candy is firm enough to form a lump for kneading. Scrape the spatulas frequently, one with the other, while working. Once the working is begun, do not stop until the mixture is creamy and starts to lose its gloss; otherwise it may become grainy.

3. Working chocolate fudge with spatulas

Kneading gives the candy a more creamy texture, but overkneading makes it too soft. To knead, gather the lump of candy and fold it over toward you. Press away from you with the heel of your hand. Usually only a few strokes are enough. When the candy is to stand longer than overnight, kneading is not necessary because the candy will soften while standing.

If the candy has been slightly overcooked and is too stiff to knead, you can either add a little water, or cream a few drops at a time and knead the liquid in, or else cover the lump of candy with a hot damp towel and let it stand for 15 to 20 minutes.

Some candies must "ripen" to mellow the flavor and produce a finer texture. All creamed candies, except orientals, to be used for chocolate coating should stand covered for at least an hour to ripen before being molded into shapes.

Most creamed candies may be kept for weeks if they are tightly covered and stored at refrigerator temperature. When removing the candy from the refrigerator, let it stand for several hours to warm to room temperature before you uncover it. This prevents moisture from collecting on the candy from the sudden change in temperature.

If any creamed candy, except orientals, is too grainy or otherwise incorrectly cooked when it is finished, it may be cooked again. Add a small amount of water to the candy in the pan, stir it over a moderate heat until it is dissolved, and cook it again to the proper degree.

## BASIC VANILLA CREAMS

2 cups sugar
1 cup 18% cream
2 tablespoons light corn sirup

¼ teaspoon salt
1 teaspoon vanilla
½ cup chopped nutmeats, if desired

1. In 2-quart saucepan, mix sugar, cream, corn sirup, and salt.

2. Stir over moderate heat until sugar is dissolved and boiling starts.
3. Cook, without stirring, to 236°F on candy thermometer (soft-ball stage).
4. Pour on lightly buttered marble slab or platter.
5. Cool to lukewarm or cooler.
6. Add vanilla and work with candy spatulas until firm enough to handle. Add nutmeats, if used.
7. Knead until creamy. Do not overknead—just a few strokes may be enough.
8. Wrap in wax paper and keep tightly covered until ready to use for chocolate-dipped centers.

## Variations

VANILLA CREAM FUDGE
1. Cook Basic Vanilla Creams to 238°F on candy thermometer (soft-ball stage).
2. Pour on buttered marble slab or platter.
3. Cool to lukewarm, or mixture may be cooled in pan in which it has been cooked.
4. Work candy with candy spatulas or beat with wooden spoons, adding vanilla and nutmeats only when it starts to lose its gloss. Lift candy from slab or pan into wax-paper-lined pan. Pat to depth of $\frac{1}{2}''$. Cut when set.
5. If fudge is to be kept more than 2 days, tightly cover and store in refrigerator to keep firm. When removing fudge from refrigerator, keep covered until it warms to room temperature.

OPERA FUDGE
1. Cook Basic Vanilla Creams to 236°F on candy thermometer (soft-ball stage).
2. Add $\frac{1}{4}$ cup 18% cream. Continue to cook, stirring frequently, to 238°F on candy thermometer (soft-ball stage).
3. Pour on buttered marble slab or platter.

4. Cool to lukewarm and work, adding vanilla and nut-meats, until creamy, or mixture may be cooled in pan in which it has been cooked.
5. Work with candy spatulas or wooden spoon until it starts to lose its gloss.
6. Pour or pat out in wax-paper-lined pan to depth of $\frac{1}{2}''$. Cut when cold.

BITTERSWEET FROSTED FUDGE
1. Spread cooled, unsweetened chocolate on top of Vanilla Cream Fudge or Opera Fudge after the fudge has been put in wax-paper-lined pan.
2. Cut into pieces when chocolate will hold marking and before it has completely hardened.

## BASIC CHOCOLATE FUDGE

2 cups sugar
1 cup 18% cream
$\frac{1}{4}$ teaspoon salt
2 tablespoons light corn
sirup or honey

2 1-ounce squares melted or
grated unsweetened chocolate
$\frac{1}{2}$ teaspoon vanilla

1. In 2-quart saucepan, mix sugar, cream, salt, and corn sirup or honey.
2. Stir over moderate heat until sugar is dissolved and boiling starts.
3. Cook, without stirring, to 236°F on candy thermometer (soft-ball stage).
4. Pour on buttered marble slab or platter.
5. Pour melted chocolate, or sprinkle grated chocolate, over candy. Do not stir.
6. When lukewarm, add vanilla.
7. Work with candy spatulas until creamy. Knead a few strokes.
9. Pat out in wax-paper-lined pan to depth of $\frac{1}{2}''$. Cut when set.

4. Pouring melted chocolate on candy for chocolate fudge

5. Chocolate fudge after working

Note: Fudge may be cooled and beaten in pan in which it has been cooked. Remove pan from heat. Drop in whole squares of chocolate. Cool mixture to lukewarm. Beat with wooden spoon until mixture starts to lose its gloss. Pour in wax-paper-lined pan, or knead candy and pat in pan, and cut when cool.

## Variations

OLD-FASHIONED FUDGE (with more pronounced grain)
1. Start creaming Basic Chocolate Fudge at warmer temperature—about 150°F.

QUICK 'N EASY FUDGE
1. Increase amount of corn sirup in Basic Chocolate Fudge to ½ cup light corn sirup.
2. Cook mixture to 236°F on candy thermometer (soft-ball stage).
3. Remove from heat. Drop in 2 1-ounce squares of chocolate and stir until mixture starts to lose its gloss.
4. Pour in wax-paper-lined pan. Cut when set.

FOR CREAMS TO BE DIPPED IN CHOCOLATE
1. Cook Basic Chocolate Fudge to 234°F on candy thermometer (soft-ball stage).
2. Cool to lukewarm. Add vanilla and 1 teaspoon glycerin.
3. Work until firm enough to handle. Knead until creamy.
4. Wrap in wax paper and store tightly covered until ready to by molded into shapes.

PENUCHE FUDGE
1. Use 1 cup firmly packed light brown sugar and 1 cup granulated sugar in place of 2 cups granulated sugar in Basic Chocolate Fudge.

ALMOND-FLAVORED FUDGE
1. Use desired amount almond extract in place of vanilla in Basic Chocolate Fudge.

Nut Fudge or Peanut Butter Fudge

1. Add ½ cup chopped nutmeats or ½ cup peanut butter near the end of creaming Basic Chocolate Fudge.

Marshmallow Fudge

1. Add 8–10 finely cut marshmallows at the end of creaming Basic Chocolate Fudge.

Chocolate Milk Fudge

1. Use 1 cup milk, or evaporated milk diluted to milk consistency, and 2–3 tablespoons butter or margarine in place of 1 cup cream in Basic Chocolate Fudge.
2. Follow directions for Basic Chocolate Fudge. Some stirring during cooking will be necessary, especially when using evaporated milk. Mixture may curdle slightly, but curdling works out in process of creaming.

## DATE FUDGE

| | |
|---|---|
| *2 cups sugar* | *1 cup finely-cut pitted dates* |
| *1 cup 18% cream* | *½ cup coarsely chopped nutmeats* |
| *¼ teaspoon salt* | |

1. In heavy 2-quart saucepan, mix sugar, cream, and salt.
2. Stir over moderate heat until sugar is dissolved and boiling starts.
3. Add dates. Continue to cook, stirring constantly, to 236°F on candy thermometer (soft-ball stage).
4. Remove from heat and stir until creamy. Add nutmeats.
5. Pat out in wax-paper-lined pan. Cut when set. Or fudge may be shaped in a log about 1″ in diameter, rolled in wax paper, and sliced as used.
6. Store tightly covered.

**Variation**

Date-Orange Fudge

1. Mix ¼ cup thawed frozen orange juice concentrate with sugar in Date Fudge. Then add cream and salt.

## PENUCHE

| 1 cup firmly packed light brown sugar | 2 teaspoons light corn sirup |
| 1 cup granulated sugar | ¼ teaspoon salt |
| 1 cup 18% cream | ½ cup chopped nutmeats, if desired |

1. In 2-quart saucepan, mix all ingredients except nutmeats.
2. Stir over moderate heat until sugar is dissolved and boiling starts.
3. Cook, without stirring, to 236°F on candy thermometer (soft-ball stage).
4. Pour on buttered marble slab or platter, or mixture may be cooled in pan in which it has been cooked.
5. Cool to lukewarm and work until creamy. Add nutmeats, if used. Work with candy spatula or beat with wooden spoon until mixture starts to lose its gloss.
6. Pour or pat out in wax-paper-lined pan to depth of ½". For fudge, cut when cold. For centers to be dipped in chocolate, keep in tightly covered container until ready to be molded into shapes.

## PENUCHE PUDDING

| 3 cups firmly packed light brown sugar | ½ cup blanched, chopped toasted almonds |
| 1½ cups 18% cream | ½ cup chopped walnuts |
| 2 tablespoons butter | ¼ cup diced candied cherries |
| ¼ teaspoon salt | ¼ cup diced candied pineapple |

1. In 3-quart saucepan, mix sugar, cream, butter, and salt.
2. Stir over moderate heat until sugar is dissolved and boiling starts.
3. Cook, without stirring, to 236°F on candy thermometer (soft-ball stage).
4. Pour on buttered marble slab or platter.
5. Cool to lukewarm. Work mixture with candy spatulas

until it starts to get creamy. Mixture may be cooled in pan in which it has been cooked and beaten with wooden spoon until it loses its gloss.

6. Add nutmeats and fruit and blend well.
7. For fudge, pat out in wax-paper-lined pan and cut. For chocolate dipping, keep in tightly covered container to mold into shapes.

## COCOA VEGETABLE OIL FUDGE

| | |
|---|---|
| 2 cups sugar | ½ cup vegetable oil |
| ⅓ cup non-fat dry milk | 2 tablespoons honey |
| ¼ cup cocoa | 1 cup water |
| ¼ teaspoon salt | 1 teaspoon vanilla |

1. In 2-quart saucepan, mix sugar, dry milk, cocoa, and salt. Add vegetable oil, honey, and water. Mix well.
2. Stir over moderate heat until sugar is dissolved and boiling starts.
3. Continue to cook to 236°F on candy thermometer (soft-ball stage).
4. Pour on buttered marble slab or platter. Cool to lukewarm.
5. Add vanilla. Work until creamy. Mixture may be cooled in pan in which it has been cooked and beaten with wooden spoon until it loses its gloss.
6. Pour or press out in wax-paper-lined pan and cut when set.

## CARAMEL FUDGE

| | |
|---|---|
| ⅓ cup sugar | ¼ cup butter or margarine |
| ¼ cup hot water | ¼ teaspoon salt |
| 1⅔ cups sugar | ½ cup coarsely chopped |
| ½ cup evaporated milk | nutmeats, if desired |

1. In heavy 2- quart saucepan or iron skillet, melt the ⅓ cup sugar over high heat, stirring constantly with wooden spoon until all sugar is just barely melted and

a golden brown, but no longer because sugar burns easily.

2. Quickly add hot water. Stir and cook until just blended.
3. Remove from heat. Replace wooden spoon with a clean wooden spoon. Dip out any remaining sugar crystals, which may adhere to the spoon in the process of melting the sugar.
4. Add all remaining ingredients except nutmeats.
5. Stir over moderate heat until sugar is dissolved and boiling starts.
6. Cook over moderate heat, stirring frequently, to 236°F on candy thermometer (soft-ball stage).
7. Remove from heat and let stand in pan until mixture is lukewarm.
8. Beat with wooden spoon until mixture begins to lose its gloss, or mixture may be poured on buttered marble slab and worked with candy spatulas. Add nutmeats if used.
9. Pour or pat in wax-paper-lined pan. Cut when set.
10. Store in tightly covered container.

Note: If a more pronounced grain is desired, work or beat mixture when warmer than lukewarm.

## MAPLE FUDGE (CREAMS)

*1 cup granulated sugar*
*1 cup light brown sugar*
*½ cup maple sirup*
*1 cup 18% cream*

*⅛ teaspoon salt*
*½ cup or more chopped nutmeats, if desired*

1. In 2-quart saucepan, combine all ingredients except nutmeats.
2. Stir over moderate heat until sugar is dissolved and boiling starts.
3. Cook, without stirring, to 238°F on candy thermometer (soft-ball stage).
4. Pour on buttered marble slab or platter.

5. Cool to lukewarm. Work until creamy. Add nutmeats, if used. Mixture may be cooled in pan in which it has been cooked and beaten with wooden spoon until mixture loses its gloss.
6. Pour or pat in wax-paper-lined pan. Cut for fudge or keep tightly covered for chocolate coating.

## Variations

### MAPLE SIRUP FUDGE

*2 cups maple sirup*

1. Pour maple sirup into 2-quart saucepan.
2. Boil to 238°F on candy thermometer (soft-ball stage).
3. Pour on buttered marble slab or platter.
4. Cool to lukewarm. Work until creamy. Mixture may be cooled in pan in which it has been cooked and beaten with wooden spoon until mixture loses its gloss.
5. Pour or pat in wax-paper-lined pan. Cut for fudge.

### MAPLE CREAM FUDGE

*2 cups maple sirup          1 cup 18% cream*

1. In 2-quart saucepan, combine maple sirup and cream.
2. Follow directions for Maple Sirup Fudge.

## FONDANT

Fondant is the basis for many varieties of candy. It is a relatively simple combination of ingredients and easily made.

## BASIC FONDANT

*2 cups sugar                ⅛ teaspoon salt*
*⅔ cup water                 flavoring desired*
*2 tablespoons light corn sirup*

1. In 2-quart saucepan, mix thoroughly all ingredients except flavoring.
2. Stir over moderate heat until sugar is dissolved and boiling starts.

3. Cover saucepan and boil 2–3 minutes.
4. Uncover. Wipe down crystals from sides of pan with cloth wrapped around tines of fork and dipped in hot water. Wipe down several times during cooking.
5. Continue boiling, without stirring, to 238°F on candy thermometer (soft-ball stage).
6. Pour on marble slab or platter which has been wiped with cold, damp cloth.
7. When lukewarm, add flavoring.
8. Work with candy spatulas until fondant is firm enough to handle and knead until creamy.
9. Store in tightly covered container. Let stand at room temperature at least several hours to ripen, but 2–4 days is better. Basic fondant can be kept stored in refrigerator for weeks.

## Uses for Basic Fondant

MINT PATTIES
1. Melt Basic Fondant (1 cup at a time is best) in small pan or double boiler over hot, not boiling, water.
2. Add coloring if used and flavoring in desired amounts as fondant melts. If fondant is too thick, add a few drops of hot water. If fondant becomes too thin, let it stand over hot water 5–10 minutes.
3. Quickly drop small patties from tip of teaspoon onto wax paper, or use warm funnel and stick.
4. When patties are dry, which takes 5–10 minutes, remove from wax paper.
5. Store in tightly covered container.

## MARZIPAN

| | |
|---|---|
| 1 cup Basic Fondant | 1 teaspoon glycerin |
| $\frac{3}{4}$–1 cup almond paste | 2 tablespoons marshmallow creme |
| $\frac{1}{2}$ teaspoon vanilla | |

1. Blend almond paste, vanilla, glycerin, and marshmallow creme into fondant.

2. If marzipan mixture seems dry, add small amount of light corn sirup. If mixture seems too moist, add confectioners' sugar.
3. Roll marzipan in balls and dip in chocolate or melted fondant.

Note: Almond paste may be made* or purchased from confectioners' supply houses or in some grocery stores.

## *ALMOND PASTE

2 cups thoroughly dried
   blanched almonds
1⅛ cups sifted confec-
   tioners' sugar

¼ cup egg whites
2 teaspoons almond extract

1. Grind blanched and thoroughly dried (not toasted) almonds through finest knife of food grinder. Then grind twice more.
2. Mix in sifted confectioners' sugar and blend in unbeaten egg whites and almond extract.
3. Mold into ball.
4. Let age in tightly covered container in refrigerator at least 4 days.

## BONBONS

centers to be dipped
1 cup Basic Fondant
1 teaspoon vanilla

½ teaspoon glycerin
coloring, if desired

1. Before melting fondant, have bonbon centers molded or cut ready for dipping. Use any center which is firm enough to handle in hot fondant—marzipan, coconut, fruit mixtures, or almost any creamed candy.
2. Melt fondant (1 cup at a time if recipe is increased) in small pan over hot, not boiling, water. Stir gently. If fondant is too thin, let stand over hot water a few minutes. If too thick, add a few drops of hot water.

3. Add vanilla, glycerin, and coloring if used as fondant melts.
4. Drop piece to be coated in melted fondant. With fork or bonbon dipper, quickly roll it in fondant to cover.
5. Remove and place on wax paper, turning fork or dipper over to let piece drop.
6. When dry, remove from paper.
7. Store tightly covered.

## CHOCOLATE-COATED MARASCHINO CHERRIES

| | |
|---|---|
| *1 cup Basic Fondant* | *maraschino cherries, well drained* |
| *1 teaspoon vanilla* | *melted, cooled dark sweet* |
| *½ teaspoon glycerin* | *chocolate or* |
| *coloring, if desired* | *milk chocolate* |

1. Drain maraschino cherries and let stand on paper towels for several hours to dry thoroughly.
2. Follow Bonbons directions for melting fondant.
3. Dip cherries in melted fondant.
4. When dry and cool, coat bottom of each piece with chocolate. Let dry and dip entire piece in chocolate. Because cherries soften fondant as it ripens, there is less leakage with double coating of chocolate on the bottom.
5. Store all chocolate-dipped cherries tightly covered and let ripen at least one week before using.

### Variation

BRANDIED CHERRIES
1. Soak well-drained maraschino cherries in Chocolate-Coated Maraschino Cherries in brandy at least 12–14 hours.
2. Drain and let stand on paper towels several hours to dry thoroughly.

# BASIC BUTTER FONDANT (CREAMS)

| | |
|---|---|
| 3 cups sugar | 1 teaspoon glycerin |
| ⅛ teaspoon cream of tartar | 1 cup water |
| 2 tablespoons light corn sirup | ¼ teaspoon salt |
| | ¼ cup butter |
| | flavoring desired |

1. In 2-quart saucepan, blend sugar, cream of tartar, corn sirup, glycerin, water, and salt.
2. Stir over moderate heat until sugar is dissolved and boiling starts.
3. Cover saucepan. Let boil 2–3 minutes.
4. Uncover. Wipe down crystals from sides of pan with cloth wrapped around tines of fork and dipped in hot water. Wipe down crystals several times during cooking.
5. Continue boiling, without stirring, to 236°F on candy thermometer (soft-ball stage).
6. Pour on damp marble slab or platter.
7. When candy is lukewarm, add butter and flavoring.
8. Work with candy spatulas until creamy.
9. Wrap in wax paper and allow to stand 1–2 hours at room temperature.
10. Mold into shapes and dip in chocolate.

Note: When doubling recipe, do not double amount of cream of tartar.

## Variations

MILK FONDANT

1. Use 1 cup milk in place of 1 cup water in Basic Butter Fondant.
2. Use a 3-quart saucepan.
3. Do not cover while cooking.

VANILLA FONDANT

1. Add 2 teaspoons vanilla to Basic Butter Fondant when starting to work candy.

VANILLA-NUT FONDANT
  1. Add 2 teaspoons vanilla and 1 cup finely chopped nutmeats to Basic Butter Fondant at end of creaming.

COCONUT FONDANT
  1. Add 2 teaspoons vanilla and $1\frac{1}{2}$ cups finely shredded coconut to Basic Butter Fondant at end of creaming.

CHOCOLATE FONDANT
  1. Add 3–4 1-ounce squares of cooled, melted unsweetened chocolate and 1 teaspoon vanilla to Basic Butter Fondant when starting to work candy.

COFFEE FONDANT
  1. Sprinkle 3–4 teaspoons instant coffee over Basic Butter Fondant as soon as it is poured on marble slab.

MOCHA FONDANT
  1. Add 2 1-ounce squares melted unsweetened chocolate and 2 teaspoons instant coffee to Basic Butter Fondant as soon as it is poured on marble slab.

FRUIT-FLAVORED FONDANT
  1. Flavor Basic Butter Fondant with desired amount of any fruit flavoring when starting to work candy. Use extracts or oils.

## FRUIT FONDANT (CREAMS)

| | |
|---|---|
| *$1\frac{1}{2}$ cups sugar* | *$\frac{1}{2}$ teaspoon glycerin* |
| *$\frac{1}{2}$ cup cream* | *2 tablespoons butter* |
| *$\frac{1}{8}$ teaspoon salt* | |

Add any of the following:
*2 tablespoons raspberry or strawberry purée*
*3 tablespoons frozen orange juice concentrate*
*$\frac{1}{4}$ cup crushed, not-drained pineapple*
*$\frac{1}{3}$ cup apricot purée*

  1. Make raspberry or strawberry purée by mashing fresh or frozen berries. Make apricot purée by mashing

cooked dried apricots. Use juice and pulp to make thin purées, which are preferable.

2. In heavy 2-quart saucepan, mix sugar, cream, salt, glycerin, and butter.
3. Stir over moderate heat until sugar is dissolved and boiling starts.
4. Cook, without stirring, to 230°F on candy thermometer.
5. Add fruit desired and continue to cook, stirring continuously to keep fruit from sticking to pan, to 238°F (soft-ball stage).
6. Pour on buttered marble slab or platter.
7. Cool to slightly warmer than lukewarm (120°F–130°F).
8. Work with candy spatulas until creamy. This takes longer than most other creamed candy.
9. Wrap in wax paper. Let ripen for 1–2 hours. Mold for bonbons or chocolate dipping.

Note: If a stronger flavor is desired, add a few drops of flavoring desired while creaming candy. Do not add more fruit because too much acid makes a candy too soft to cream.

## ORIENTALS

Orientals are a more sophisticated type of fondant. With the addition of beaten egg which adds air and some moisture, orientals ripen more quickly. They will need to be finished within a few hours after they are started.

### BASIC ORIENTALS

*3 cups sugar*
*1 cup water*
*2 tablespoons light corn sirup*
*⅛ teaspoon (scant) cream of tartar*

*1 teaspoon glycerin*
*⅛ teaspoon salt*
*1 medium egg white*
*flavoring desired*
*coloring, if desired*

1. In 2-quart saucepan, mix sugar, water, corn sirup, cream of tartar, glycerin, and salt.
2. Stir over moderate heat until sugar is dissolved and boiling starts.
3. Cover pan and let boil 2–3 minutes.
4. Uncover. Wipe down sugar crystals from sides of pan with cloth wrapped around tines of fork and dipped in hot water. Wipe down crystals several times during cooking.
5. Cook, without stirring, to 240°F–242°F on candy thermometer (soft-ball stage).
6. Pour on cold damp marble slab.
7. Cool to lukewarm.
8. Add stiffly beaten egg white, flavoring, and coloring if used.
9. Work with candy spatulas until creamy. This takes much longer than most other creamed candies and for a while may not appear to be creaming.
10. Let stand 10–15 minutes to set. Mold into desired shapes for chocolate coating. A small amount of cornstarch may be used on hands to make molding easier. If pieces of candy seem soft, place on wax paper which has been lightly dusted with cornstarch.
11. When thin crust has formed on shaped pieces, which takes about 20–30 minutes, dip in chocolate.

Note: When doubling recipe, do not double amount of cream of tartar.

### Variations

BUTTER ORIENTALS
1. Add ¼ cup butter when starting to cook Basic Orientals.
2. Do not cover pan while boiling.

PEPPERMINT ORIENTALS
1. Add ¼ teaspoon (scant) oil of peppermint when starting to work Basic Orientals.

WINTERGREEN ORIENTALS
1. Add ¼ teaspoon oil of wintergreen and a few drops red coloring (to make mixture pink) when starting to work Basic Orientals.

OTHER FLAVORINGS FOR BOTH BASIC AND BUTTER ORIENTALS
1. Choose from the flavoring listed under variations of Basic Butter Fondant (page 32). Add in same amounts.

## FRUIT ORIENTALS

| | |
|---|---|
| 3 cups sugar | ⅛ teaspoon salt |
| 1 cup water | 1 medium egg white |
| 1 teaspoon glycerin | |

Add any of the following:

| | |
|---|---|
| ¼ cup raspberry purée | 6 tablespoons frozen orange juice |
| ¼ cup strawberry purée | concentrate |
| ½ cup crushed pineapple | ⅔ cup apricot purée |

1. Make raspberry or strawberry purée by mashing fresh or frozen berries. Make apricot purée by mashing cooked dried apricots. Crushed pineapple should not be drained.
2. In heavy 2-quart saucepan, mix sugar, water, glycerin, and salt.
3. Stir over moderate heat until sugar is dissolved and boiling starts.
4. Cook, without stirring, to 230°F on candy thermometer.
5. Add fruit desired and continue to cook, stirring continuously to keep fruit from sticking to pan, to 240°F–242°F on candy thermometer (barely firm-ball stage).
6. Pour on cold damp slab or platter. Cool to slightly warmer than lukewarm (120°F–130°F). Add beaten egg white and work with candy spatulas until creamy, which may take 30 minutes.
7. Let stand 10–15 minutes to set. Mold into desired shapes for chocolate coating. Follow directions for molding as given under Basic Orientals (page 34).

# DIVINITY, NOUGAT, AND MARSHMALLOWS

Texture is the important word in divinity, nougat, and marshmallows. These candies are made by incorporating air in the process of beating by using egg whites or gelatin.

Because divinity and marshmallows have a light fluffy texture, they are an especially good summertime candy. They are easily made and less rich than other types of candies. Properly stored, they keep at least a week. Nougat is slightly heavier in texture and will keep for months, wrapped or dipped and properly stored.

An electric beater is essential in making nougat and marshmallows, though divinities can be successfully made with a hand beater.

## BASIC DIVINITY

| | |
|---|---|
| 2 cups sugar | ¼ cup egg whites |
| ½ cup light corn sirup | 1 teaspoon vanilla |
| ½ cup water | ½ cup chopped nutmeats |
| ⅛ teaspoon salt | |

1. In 2-quart saucepan, mix thoroughly sugar, corn sirup, and water.

2. Stir over moderate heat until sugar is dissolved and boiling starts.
3. Cook, without stirring, to 258°F-260°F on candy thermometer (hard-ball stage).
4. Remove from heat and let stand while beating egg whites.
5. Combine salt and egg whites. Beat until stiff peaks form.
6. Pour cooked mixture slowly over egg whites, beating continuously.
7. Continue beating until candy loses its gloss and will retain shape when dropped from spoon. First part of beating may be done with hand beater, then use heavy spoon as mixture gets heavier.
8. Add flavoring during last part of beating. Blend in nutmeats with spoon.
9. Drop pieces the size of a teaspoon on wax paper or buttered cookie sheet, or candy may be poured in one piece and cut when set.
10. Store in tightly covered container.

Note: Divinity may be colored and flavored as desired while beating.

## Variations

FRESH-FRUIT-FLAVORED DIVINITY

1. Cook Basic Divinity to 270°F-272°F on candy thermometer (soft-crack stage).
2. Pour mixture slowly over stiffly beaten eggs whites, beating continuously.
3. For Orange Divinity, add 1 tablespoon frozen orange juice concentrate during last part of beating.
4. For Raspberry or Strawberry Divinity, add 2 tablespoons raspberry or strawberry purée, made by mashing frozen or fresh fruit, during last part of beating.

# BROWN SUGAR DIVINITY (SEA FOAM)

*1 cup firmly packed light
    brown sugar*
*1 cup granulated sugar*
*¼ cup light corn sirup*
*¾ cup water*

*¼ cup egg whites*
*⅛ teaspoon salt*
*1 teaspoon vanilla*
*½ cup chopped nutmeats*

1. In 2-quart saucepan, combine sugars, corn sirup, and water.
2. Stir over moderate heat until sugars are dissolved and boiling starts.
3. Cook, without stirring, to 258°F-260°F on candy thermometer (hard-ball stage).
4. Remove from heat and let stand while beating egg whites.
5. Combine salt and egg whites and beat until stiff peaks form.
6. Pour cooked mixture slowly into egg whites, beating continuously.
7. Continue beating until candy loses its gloss and holds its shape when dropped from a spoon.
8. Add flavoring during the latter part of beating. Blend in nutmeats with a spoon.
9. Drop pieces the size of a teaspoon on wax paper or buttered cookie sheet, or pour all the candy in a buttered pan and cut when set.

## BASIC NOUGAT

*1 cup sugar*
*¾ cup light corn sirup*
*¼ cup water*
*⅛ teaspoon salt*
*1 medium egg white*
*2 tablespoons honey*

*2 tablespoons butter*
*1 teaspoon vanilla*
*½ cup chopped pistachio
    nutmeats*
*½ cup coarsely cut
    candied cherries*

1. In 2-quart saucepan, combine sugar, corn sirup, water, and salt.
2. Stir over moderate heat until sugar is dissolved and boiling starts.
3. Cook, without stirring, to 295°F on candy thermometer (hard-crack stage).
4. While sirup is cooking, beat egg white until soft peaks form. Gradually add honey a little at a time and beat in thoroughly.
5. Pour cooked sirup slowly into egg white mixture, beating continuously with electric beater. Add butter, small amounts at a time.
6. Continue beating until mixture is thick and heavy. Add vanilla.
7. Remove beaters. Mix in nutmeats and fruit with spoon.
8. Pour into buttered pan to depth of $\frac{1}{2}''$.
9. Let stand several hours or overnight to set.
10. Turn out on lightly buttered board or marble slab. If nougat sticks to bottom of pan, hold it over low heat for a few seconds.
11. Cut, using sawing motion. Wrap each piece in wax paper, or dip in chocolate.

Note: For a firmer nougat, use 1 cup corn sirup instead of $\frac{3}{4}$ cup.

## Variations

ALMOND NOUGAT
1. Use $\frac{3}{4}$ cup blanched, whole or chopped, toasted almonds in place of the pistachio nutmeats and cherries in Basic Nougat.

GUM DROP NOUGAT
1. Use $\frac{1}{2}$ cup chopped gum drops in place of the pistachio nutmeats and cherries in Basic Nougat.

## FLUFFY NOUGAT

2 cups sugar
½ cup water
½ cup light corn sirup
⅛ teaspoon salt

1 egg white
1 tablespoon honey
1 teaspoon vanilla

1. In 2-quart saucepan, combine sugar, water, corn sirup, and salt.
2. Stir over moderate heat until sugar is dissolved.
3. Cook, without stirring, to 280°F on candy thermometer (soft-crack stage).
4. Meanwhile, beat egg white until soft peaks form. Add honey slowly and beat in thoroughly.
5. Pour cooked sirup slowly into egg white mixture, beating continuously with electric beater.
6. Continue to beat until mixture is thick and lukewarm. Add vanilla during latter part of beating.
7. Pour in buttered pan to depth of about ½".
8. Let stand overnight. Cut. Use nougat for Caramel Balls or Logs (page 54).

Note: Chopped fruit and/or nuts may be stirred in after nougat mixture is beaten until thick and lukewarm. In this case, cut and wrap, or dip in chocolate.

## NOUGATINE

1 cup sugar
⅔ cup light corn sirup
⅛ teaspoon salt
2 tablespoons butter
¼ cup marshmallow creme

¼ cup finely chopped candied cherries
¼ cup coarsely chopped toasted almonds
1 teaspoon vanilla

1. In 1-quart saucepan, mix sugar, corn sirup, and salt.
2. Stir over moderate heat until sugar is dissolved and boiling starts.
3. Cook, without stirring, to 270°F–272°F on candy thermometer (soft-crack stage).

4. Remove from heat. Add butter and stir until blended. Add remaining ingredients and mix thoroughly.
5. Pour in buttered pan to depth of $\frac{1}{2}''$.
6. When cold, cut and wrap in wax paper, or coat with chocolate.

## BASIC MARSHMALLOWS

| | |
|---|---|
| $\frac{1}{4}$ cup cold water | $\frac{1}{2}$ cup water |
| 1 tablespoon gelatin | 1 teaspoon vanilla |
| 1 cup sugar | coloring, if desired |
| $\frac{1}{2}$ cup light corn sirup | confectioners' sugar |

1. In electric mixing bowl, combine $\frac{1}{4}$ cup cold water and gelatin. Let stand at least 5 minutes.
2. In 1-quart saucepan, combine sugar, corn sirup, and another $\frac{1}{4}$ cup water.
3. Stir over moderate heat until sugar is dissolved and boiling starts.
4. Cook, without stirring, to 242°F–244°F on candy thermometer (firm-ball stage).
5. Slowly pour cooked mixture into softened gelatin, beating continuously with electric mixer. Continue beating until mixture is fluffy, white, and lukewarm. This takes about 5 minutes.
6. Add flavoring and coloring if used.
7. Pour to depth of about $\frac{3}{4}''$ in pan which has been lightly buttered and dusted with confectioners' sugar.
8. Let stand overnight.
9. Sprinkle top of candy with confectioners' sugar. Lightly butter and dust knife or candy spatula with confectioners' sugar. Loosen sides and bottom of candy and turn out on cookie sheet which has been thickly coated with confectioners' sugar.
10. Keeping knife, candy spatula, or scissors well coated with confectioners' sugar, cut marshmallow in strips, then into small pieces. When cutting, press knife down

through—do not draw knife through marshmallow. Roll each piece of candy in sugar, keeping hands well coated with sugar.

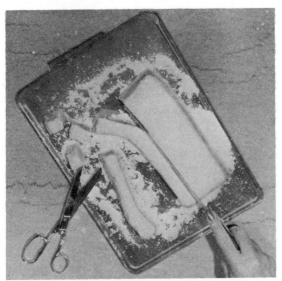

6. Cutting marshmallows

11. Store tightly covered.

## Variation

FRUIT MARSHMALLOWS
1. Use $\frac{1}{4}$ cup any cold fruit juice, except fresh pineapple, in place of $\frac{1}{4}$ cup cold water in Basic Marshmallows to soften gelatin.

## Uses for Basic Marshmallows

JELLY MARSHMALLOWS
1. Pour layer of Basic Marshmallows to depth of about

$\frac{1}{4}''$ over previously made gelatin jelly (page 46) to depth of $\frac{1}{2}''$. When combining two candies, they stick together better if one or both is warm.

2. Cut and roll in confectioners' sugar.

CARAMEL MARSHMALLOWS

1. Pour layer of Basic Marshmallows to depth of about $\frac{1}{4}''$ over previously made caramel (page 51 & 53) of equal depth. When combining two candies, they stick together better if one or both is warm.
2. Cut together and dip in chocolate.

CHOCOLATE-DIPPED MARSHMALLOWS

1. Rub excess sugar from Basic Marshmallows.
2. Dip marshmallows in chocolate.
3. Let dry or roll in finely chopped nutmeats or toasted coconut.

CHOCOLATE MARSHMALLOW FLUFF

1. Add pieces of coarsely cut Basic Marshmallows to cooled, melted semi-sweet chocolate, using just enough chocolate to coat marshmallows thoroughly. Nuts or a few drops of peppermint for flavoring may be added.
2. Pour into wax-paper-lined pan.
3. Cut when chocolate begins to dry.

TOASTED-COCONUT MARSHMALLOWS

1. Rub excess sugar from Basic Marshmallows, or commercial marshmallows may be used dipped in the following sirup.*
2. Roll marshmallows in toasted coconut. To toast coconut, spread thin layer on cookie sheet. Toast in oven preheated to 300°F. Watch closely, stirring a few times as coconut toasts to a light brown.

## *SIRUP FOR MARSHMALLOWS

$\frac{1}{2}$ cup light corn sirup          $\frac{1}{4}$ cup honey
$\frac{1}{3}$ cup sugar

1. Combine all ingredients in saucepan and bring to boil.
2. Remove from heat and let stand until lukewarm.

# JELLIES

Subtly light in flavor and texture are jellies. Sugar-coated and tart-sweet, they add interest to a candy assortment. Though just a "sometime candy," they are certainly worth making.

## BASIC GELATIN JELLY

| | |
|---|---|
| 2 tablespoons unflavored gelatin | 2 cups sugar |
| ⅓ cup lemon juice | ⅔ cup water |
| 3 tablespoons cold water | 5-6 drops yellow coloring |
| grated rind of 1 lemon | sifted confectioners' or granulated sugar |

1. Combine gelatin, lemon juice, 3 tablespoons cold water, and grated lemon rind. Let stand at least 5 minutes.
2. In heavy 3-quart saucepan, mix sugar, ⅔ cup water, and coloring.
3. Stir over moderate heat until sugar is dissolved and boiling starts. Cover and let mixture boil about 2 minutes.
4. Uncover and cook, without stirring, to 236°F on candy

thermometer. Remove from heat and add gelatin mixture.

5. Return to moderate heat and cook, stirring continuously, to 222°F–224°F. Watch closely because it may take only a few seconds after boiling starts.
6. Pour into lightly buttered pan to depth of about $\frac{1}{2}''$. Let stand overnight.
7. Sprinkle top of jelly with sifted confectioners' or granulated sugar. With knife or spatula which has been buttered and coated with sugar, release candy from pan. Turn out on sugar-coated cookie sheet.
8. To cut, press sugar-coated knife or spatula down through—do not draw knife through jelly.
9. With hands well coated with sugar, roll each piece in sugar.
10. Store tightly covered, or remove excess sugar from jelly and dip in chocolate.

Note: Jellies are more tender if allowed to stand a week or more.

## Variations

RASPBERRY OR STRAWBERRY JELLY
1. Soak gelatin in $\frac{1}{2}$ cup raspberry or strawberry purée (made by mashing fresh or frozen berries) and 1 tablespoon lemon juice instead of $\frac{1}{3}$ cup lemon juice, cold water, and lemon rind in Basic Gelatin Jelly.
2. Omit coloring in Basic Gelatin Jelly.

ORANGE JELLY

| | |
|---|---|
| 2 tablespoons unflavored gelatin | grated rind of $\frac{1}{2}$ orange, if desired |
| $\frac{1}{4}$ cup thawed frozen orange juice concentrate | 2 cups sugar |
| 2 tablespoons lemon juice | $\frac{2}{3}$ cup water |
| 2 tablespoons water | sifted confectioners' or granulated sugar |

1. Combine gelatin, orange juice concentrate, lemon

juice, water, and grated rind if used. Let stand at least 5 minutes.

2. In heavy 3-quart saucepan, mix sugar and $\frac{2}{3}$ cup water. Stir over moderate heat until sugar is dissolved and boiling starts. Cover and let mixture boil about 2 minutes

3. Uncover and cook, without stirring, to 236°F on candy thermometer. Take from heat and add gelatin mixture.

4. Return to moderate heat. Cook, stirring continuously, to 222°F–224°F. Watch closely because it may take only a few seconds after boiling starts.

5. Pour in lightly buttered pan to depth of about $\frac{1}{2}''$. Let stand overnight.

6. Sprinkle top of jelly with sifted confectioners' or granulated sugar. With knife or spatula which has been buttered and coated with sugar, release candy from pan. Turn out on sugar-coated cookie sheet.

7. To cut, press sugar-coated knife or spatula down through—do not draw knife through jelly.

8. With hands well coated with sugar, roll each piece in sugar. Store tightly covered, or remove excess sugar from jelly and dip in chocolate.

## APRICOT JELLY

| | |
|---|---|
| 1½ cups apricot pulp | ¼ cup light corn sirup |
| 1¼ cups sugar | 1 tablespoon lemon juice |

1. To make apricot pulp, steam dried apricots until soft. While hot, mash thoroughly or put through coarse sieve.

2. In heavy 2-quart saucepan, mix all ingredients.

3. Cook over low heat, stirring continuously, until thick. Small amount should be firm enough to hold its shape when dropped from spoon on plate. Apricot jelly becomes too thick to allow true test on candy thermometer.

4. Pour into buttered pan to depth of about $\frac{1}{2}''$.
5. Let stand until cold and set.
6. Cut and roll pieces in confectioners' or granulated sugar, or dip in chocolate or melted fondant.
7. Store in tightly covered container.

Note: 1 cup finely chopped walnut meats or 1 cup finely shredded coconut may be added just before jelly is poured in pan.

## DATE JELLY

| | |
|---|---|
| 1½ cups date pulp | 1 cup sugar |
| ⅓ cup thawed frozen orange juice concentrate | ⅛ teaspoon salt |
| ½ cup light corn sirup | 1 cup coarsely chopped nutmeats, if desired |

1. To make date pulp, steam dates until soft. While hot, mash or put through coarse blade of food chopper.
2. In heavy 1-quart saucepan, mix all ingredients, except nutmeats.
3. Cook over low heat, stirring continuously, until thick. Small amount should be firm enough to hold its shape when dropped from spoon on plate. Date jelly becomes too thick to allow true test with candy thermometer.
4. Add nutmeats if used. Pour jelly in buttered pan to depth of $\frac{1}{2}''$.
5. Cut when cold and set.
6. Roll in confectioners' or granulated sugar, or dip in chocolate.

Note: Dried prunes, raisins, or figs which have been steamed and mashed may by used instead of the dates, or a combination of steamed and mashed fruits may be used.

## APPLESAUCE JELLY

| | |
|---|---|
| 2 tablespoons unflavored gelatin | 2 cups sugar |
| ½ cup cold water | 1 tablespoon light corn sirup |
| 2 cups unsweetened, thick, strained applesauce | ⅛ teaspoon salt |
| | 1 cup chopped nutmeats, if desired |

1. Dissolve gelatin in cold water and let stand at least 5 minutes.
2. In heavy 2-quart saucepan, combine applesauce, sugar, and corn sirup.
3. Cook until very thick, stirring continuously. Small amount should be firm enough to hold its shape when dropped from spoon on plate. Mixture is too thick to allow true test with candy thermometer.
4. Remove from heat. Add gelatin, stirring in thoroughly. Add salt and nutmeats if used.
5. Pour in buttered pan to depth of about $\frac{1}{2}''$.
6. Let stand until firm and cut.
7. Roll in confectioners' or granulated sugar, or dip in chocolate. Small amount of cinnamon may be mixed with granulated sugar, if desired.

**Variation**

CINNAMON APPLESAUCE JELLY
1. Make the apple sauce for Applesauce Jelly by adding 2 tablespoons red cinnamon candies to apples as they cook.

# CARAMELS AND CHEWS

Perhaps the stars of the homemade candy world are the caramels. Smooth, rich, and sweet, they have a distinctive buttery flavor. To add to their appeal, they are easy to make successfully, and a basic recipe may yield many variations. Included in this section too are other popular chewy types of candy.

A candy thermometer will be a great help to you in making caramels, but it is possible to use the ball method. Caramels and chews keep extremely well when properly stored in tightly covered metal containers in a cool place.

## BASIC CREAM CARAMELS

*1 cup sugar*
*⅔ cup light corn sirup*
*¼ teaspoon salt*
*1½ cups 18% cream*

*1 teaspoon vanilla, if desired*
*½ cup chopped nutmeats,*
 *if desired*

1. In heavy 2-quart saucepan, mix sugar, corn sirup, and salt thoroughly. Add ½ cup of the cream.
2. Stir over moderate heat until mixture starts to boil.

Then cook, stirring occasionally, to 238°F–240°F on candy thermometer (soft-ball stage).

3. Add another $\frac{1}{2}$ cup of the cream and cook, stirring frequently, to 238°F–240°F (soft-ball stage).
4. Add remaining $\frac{1}{2}$ cup cream. Cook, stirring frequently, to about 232°F and then stir continuously over low to moderate heat. Cook to 240°F–242°F for a soft caramel or 244°F–246°F for a firm caramel (firm-ball stage).
5. Remove pan from heat. Let stand about 5 minutes.
6. Stir in vanilla and/or nuts if used. Pour caramel in buttered pan to depth of about $\frac{1}{2}$".
7. Let stand until cool. Turn out on wooden board or marble slab. If caramel sticks to pan in which it has been cooked, hold pan a few inches over low heat for a few minutes to release.
8. Cut in small squares using sawing motion.
9. Wrap in wax paper, or dip in chocolate.
10. Store in tightly covered container in cool place.

## Variations

SOFT RICH CARAMELS
1. Use heavier cream (about 22%) in place of the 18% cream in Basic Cream Caramels, or add $\frac{1}{4}$ cup butter in the first cooking.

CHOCOLATE CARAMELS
1. Drop 1–2 1-ounce squares unsweetened chocolate in Basic Cream Caramel mixture after removing it from heat in final cooking.
2. Let stand until chocolate is melted. Stir until blended and pour in buttered pan.

PENUCHE CARAMELS
1. Use $\frac{3}{4}$ cup firmly packed, light brown sugar and $\frac{1}{2}$ cup granulated sugar in place of the 1 cup sugar in Basic Cream Caramels.

FONDANT CARAMELS

1. Cook Basic Cream Caramels or Penuche Caramels to 240°F on candy thermometer in final cooking.
2. Remove from heat but leave thermometer in mixture. When temperature drops to about 180°F, add ½ cup previously-made Basic Fondant (page 28) which has ripened 12 hours or more.
3. Blend well. Add ½ cup chopped nutmeats if desired.
4. Pour in buttered pan to depth of about ½".
5. Cut when cold and wrap, or dip in chocolate.

## MILK CARAMELS

| | |
|---|---|
| 1 cup sugar | ½ teaspoon vanilla, if |
| ⅔ cup light corn sirup | desired |
| ¼ teaspoon salt | ½ cup chopped nutmeats, |
| ¼ cup butter or margarine | if desired |
| 1½ cups milk | |

1. In heavy 2-quart saucepan, mix sugar, corn sirup, and salt.
2. Stir over moderate heat until boiling starts. Cook to 248°F–250°F on candy thermometer (firm-ball stage), which takes only a few minutes.
3. Add butter or margarine, stirring until melted. Add ½ cup of the milk gradually, keeping mixture boiling.
4. Cook over moderate heat, stirring continuously, to 242°F–244°F (firm-ball stage).
5. Again add ½ cup milk gradually, keeping mixture boiling, and cook, stirring continuously, over moderate heat to 242°F–244°F (firm-ball stage).
6. Add remaining ½ cup milk gradually. Cook, stirring continuously, over moderate heat to 240°F–242°F for soft caramel or 244°F–246°F for firm caramel (firm-ball stage).
7. Remove from heat and let stand about 5 minutes.
8. Stir to blend well. Add vanilla and/or nutmeats if used.

9. Pour in well-buttered pan to depth of about $\frac{1}{2}''$.
10. Let stand until cold. Turn out on wooden board or marble slab. If caramel sticks to pan in which it has been cooked, hold pan a few inches over low heat for a few minutes to release.
11. Cut in squares using sawing motion.
12. Wrap in wax paper, or dip in chocolate.
13. Store in tightly covered container in cool place.

## Variations

EVAPORATED MILK CARAMELS

1. Use $\frac{3}{4}$ cup evaporated milk in place of the $1\frac{1}{2}$ cups milk in Milk Caramels. Add $\frac{1}{4}$ cup at each of the three cookings.

CARAMEL FOR DIPPING

1. Make 1 recipe of Basic Cream or Milk Caramels.
2. When caramel has cooked to 240°F–242°F in final cooking, keep mixture hot, but not boiling, over very low heat. Caramel mixture must be kept hot to be thin enough for dipping. If at any time caramel gets too thick for dipping, reheat over low heat.

## Uses for Caramels

CARAMEL PECAN BALLS AND LOGS

1. Have ready 1 recipe Fluffy Nougat (page 41), made with or without nuts or fruit. The nougat is better for this purpose if it is at least a day old.
2. Roll nougat in small balls or shape into logs about 2″ long and $\frac{3}{4}''$ in diameter. Place on wax paper or buttered cookie sheet. Let nougat stand so that a slight crust forms.
3. Prepare Caramel for Dipping. Keep mixture hot.
4. Put halves or coarsely chopped nutmeats in piles on cookie sheet which should be placed next to pan of hot caramel on the stove.
5. Drop one piece of nougat at a time into the hot caramel.

Quickly coat nougat with caramel, using fork or fondant dipper.

7. Making caramel pecan balls

6. Remove coated nougat to pile of nuts on cookie sheet and roll in nuts to cover.
7. Let stand until cold. Store in tightly covered container. If nougat is shaped in small logs, wrap each log in wax paper for storing. When serving, cut each log into $\frac{1}{2}''$ slices.

Note: You can make Caramel Pecan Balls and Logs by yourself, but a helper is most useful. One person may then dip nougat in caramel, and the other, roll pieces in nuts.

CARAMEL NUT NUGGETS
1. Make 1 recipe of Basic Cream or Milk Caramels. Cook

mixture to 240°F–242°F on candy thermometer (firm-ball stage).

2. Pour caramel in buttered pan and let stand until cold.
3. Cut thin strips of caramel the size to cover 1 or 2 pecan halves or 1 large toasted almond (about $\frac{1}{8}''$ thick, $\frac{1}{2}''$ wide, and $2''$ long).
4. Roll pecan halves or almonds in strips of caramel, leaving ends of nuts showing.
5. Add cooled melted chocolate to top and bottom, or coat entire piece with chocolate.

CARAMEL PECAN PATTIES

1. Make 1 recipe of Basic Cream or Milk Caramels. Cook mixture to 240°F–242°F on candy thermometer (firm-ball stage).
2. When caramel is cooking, butter cookie sheet and place small piles of pecans on it (4–5 pecan halves in each) $1''$–$2''$ apart.
3. When caramel is cooked, drop small amount on each pile of nuts, using teaspoon. If caramel becomes too thick, reheat over low heat.
4. When caramel is cold, coat top and bottom of each piece with chocolate which has been melted and cooled to dipping temperature. All milk chocolate or part milk chocolate and part dark sweet chocolate may be used. To coat, hold patty in one hand while coating the bottom with finger of other hand or with spatula which has been dipped in cooled melted chocolate. Place patty on wax paper. After all patties are coated on the bottom and the chocolate is dry so candies will not slide, coat top of patties with chocolate, leaving them on the paper.
5. Store in tightly covered container.

CEREAL BARS

1. In large buttered bowl, measure 4–6 cups ready-to-eat cereal (one kind or several kinds mixed together).

2. Cook Basic Cream or Milk Caramels to 236°F–238°F on candy thermometer (soft-ball stage).
3. Pour caramel over cereal. Mix thoroughly.
4. Pat out in buttered pan. When cold, cut in bars.
5. Store tightly covered.

CARAMEL APPLES
1. Wash, dry, and remove stems from small eating apples. Insert small wooden skewers in the stem end.
2. Holding apple by skewer, dip it in hot Caramel for Dipping and roll to cover. Lift from pan and let drip a few seconds over pan. Then place apple on buttered cookie sheet, skewer pointing up, or cool caramel coating quickly by dipping coated apple in pan of ice water for a second or two. The ice water sets the caramel so it doesn't slide to the bottom of apple, making thicker base. Caramel-coated apples may be rolled in finely ground nutmeats without dipping them first in ice water.

## MOLASSES CHEWS

| | |
|---|---|
| 1 cup granulated sugar | 1 teaspoon vinegar |
| ½ cup firmly packed, light brown sugar | ¼ cup butter or margarine |
| | ⅛ teaspoon salt |
| ¾ cup light molasses | ½ teaspoon (scant) ginger |
| ¼ cup light corn sirup | |

1. In 3-quart saucepan, combine all ingredients and mix thoroughly.
2. Stir over moderate heat until sugar is dissolved and boiling starts.
3. Cook, stirring occasionally, to 250°F–252°F on candy thermometer (hard-ball stage).
4. Pour in buttered pan to depth of about ½″.
5. When cold, cut in squares using sawing motion.
6. Wrap in wax paper, or dip pieces in chocolate.
7. Store in tightly covered container.

## Variation

MOLASSES-COCONUT CHEWS
1. Remove Molasses Chews from heat after mixture has cooked to 250°F–252°F on candy thermometer. Leave thermometer in mixture.
2. When mixture has cooled to about 180°F, add 1 cup or more finely shredded coconut. Blend in with as little stirring as possible and pour mixture in buttered pan.

## GRAPE CHEWS

*2 cups sugar*
*1 6-ounce can thawed frozen grape juice concentrate*

*1 tablespoon lemon juice*
*¼ cup butter or margarine*
*⅛ teaspoon salt*

1. In 2-quart saucepan, combine all ingredients.
2. Stir over moderate heat until sugar is dissolved and boiling starts.
3. Cook to 256°F on candy thermometer (hard-ball stage).
4. Pour in buttered pan to depth of about ½″.
5. When cold, cut in squares using sawing motion.
6. Wrap in wax paper, or dip in chocolate.
7. Store in tightly covered container.

## Variations

RASPBERRY OR PINEAPPLE CHEWS
1. Use 1 cup raspberry juice and pulp or 1 cup crushed, undrained pineapple in place of the grape concentrate in Grape Chews.
2. Some stirring during cooking may be necessary to keep fruit from sticking to pan.

ORANGE CHEWS
1. Use ½ cup thawed frozen orange juice concentrate and ½ cup light corn sirup in place of the grape concentrate in Grape Chews.

# PULLED CANDY

The title "pulled candy" may not bring memories, but what about the title "taffy?" Perhaps no candy makes us recall childhood experiences more vividly. So start a candy tradition or revive a memory—and pull some taffy!

A few facts and you are ready to pull.

The air that is incorporated into the candy in the process of pulling taffy reduces the intensity of the color and gives the candy a lighter, more elastic texture.

If taffy sticks to your fingers, dip fingertips in cornstarch and rub lightly with butter.

The time it takes to pull candy depends on the temperature of the candy, the room temperature, and the speed at which taffy is pulled.

When taffy has been pulled enough, it will show small parallel ridges and become lighter in color and texture.

### BASIC WHITE TAFFY

1 cup sugar
⅔ cup light corn sirup
1½ tablespoons butter

⅛ teaspoon salt
1 teaspoon vanilla

1. In 1-quart saucepan, mix all ingredients except vanilla. Stir over moderate heat until boiling starts.
2. Cook to 256°F–258°F on candy thermometer (hard-ball stage).
3. Pour on buttered marble slab or platter.
4. Fold outside edges to the center as candy cools to keep edges from getting too brittle to pull.
5. When cool enough to handle, add vanilla and pull until white and light in texture.

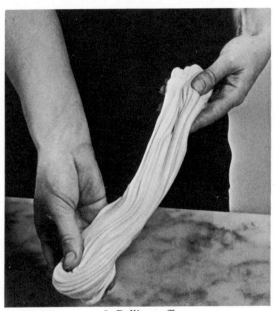

8. Pulling taffy

6. Stretch into rope about ¾″ wide on buttered cookie sheet.
7. Cut in small pieces with scissors. Let stand until cold.

8. Wrap each piece in wax paper. Store in tightly covered container.

Note: If desired, add a few drops of coloring, either as taffy cooks or when starting to pull.

## Variations

MINT TAFFY

1. Use $\frac{1}{4}$ teaspoon (scant) oil of peppermint or $\frac{1}{2}$ teaspoon (more if desired) peppermint extract in place of the vanilla in Basic White Taffy.

ORANGE OR LEMON TAFFY

1. Use 1 teaspoon orange or 1 teaspoon lemon extract in place of the vanilla in Basic White Taffy.

PECAN TAFFY

1. Add $\frac{1}{4}$ cup finely chopped pecan meats when starting to pull Basic White Taffy.

MAPLE TAFFY

1. Omit 1 cup sugar and 1 teaspoon vanilla from Basic White Taffy.
2. Add 1 cup maple sirup when mixing remaining ingredients in Basic White Taffy.

### MOLASSES TAFFY

| | |
|---|---|
| *1 cup light molasses or sorghum* | *$\frac{1}{4}$ cup butter* |
| *$\frac{1}{4}$ cup light corn sirup* | *$\frac{1}{4}$ teaspoon salt* |
| *1 cup granulted sugar* | *1 tablespoon vinegar* |
| *$\frac{1}{2}$ cup firmly packed, light brown sugar* | *$\frac{1}{8}$ teaspoon baking soda* |

1. In heavy 2-quart saucepan, combine all ingredients except baking soda.
2. Cook, stirring occasionally, to 264°F–266°F on candy thermometer (hard-ball stage).
3. Remove from heat and thoroughly stir in baking soda.
4. Pour on well-buttered marble slab or platter.

5. Fold outside edges into center as candy cools to keep edges from becoming too brittle to pull.
6. When cool enough to handle, pull until lighter in color and texture.
7. Stretch into rope about $\frac{3}{4}''$ wide on buttered cookie sheet.
8. Cut in small pieces with scissors. Butter scissors if taffy sticks. Let stand until cold.

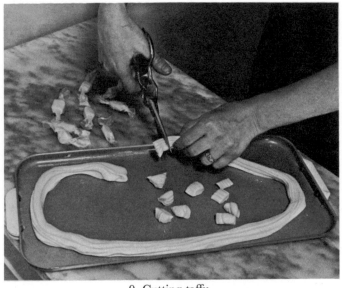

9. Cutting taffy

9. Wrap each piece in wax paper.
10. Store in tightly covered container.

## Variations

PEANUT BUTTER TAFFY

1. Cook Molasses Taffy to 266°F on candy thermometer (hard-ball stage).
2. Remove from heat. Add $\frac{1}{4}$ cup peanut butter. It is not necessary to mix peanut butter in thoroughly because it will blend while pulling.

PEANUT-BUTTER-FILLED TAFFY

1. Cook Molasses Taffy to 260°F on candy thermometer (hard-ball stage).
2. Cool and pull as directed in Molasses Taffy.
3. Flatten or roll taffy to about $\frac{1}{8}''$ thick and 3″–4″ wide.
4. Spread thin layer of peanut butter down middle of taffy. Bring two sides together, with taffy overlapping. Press firmly, shaping piece in a roll.
5. Cut in small pieces with scissors. When cold, wrap in wax paper, or let stand 1 hour or more to harden and dip in chocolate.

## HONEY AND VINEGAR TAFFY

*1 cup sugar*
*½ cup honey*
*¼ cup cider vinegar*

*1 tablespoon butter or margarine*

1. In 1-quart saucepan, combine all ingredients.
2. Stir over moderate heat until sugar is dissolved and boiling starts.
3. Cook, without stirring, to 278°F–280°F on candy thermometer (soft-crack stage).
4. Pour on well-buttered marble slab or platter.
5. Fold outside edges into center of mixture as it cools to keep edges from becoming too brittle to pull.
6. When cool enough to handle, pull until lighter in color and texture.
7. Stretch into $\frac{3}{4}''$-wide rope on buttered cookie sheet.
8. Cut into small pieces with scissors.
9. Wrap each piece in wax paper.
10. Store in tightly covered container.

## FRUIT TAFFY

1 cup sugar
¼ cup light corn sirup
Any of the following:
½ cup raspberry juice or
  purée
½ cup strawberry juice or
  purée

1 tablespoon butter or margarine
dash salt

½ cup thawed frozen grape
  juice concentrate

1. In heavy 1-quart saucepan, mix sugar, corn sirup, butter or margarine, salt, and fruit desired. Make raspberry or strawberry purée by mashing fresh or frozen berries.
2. Stir over moderate heat until sugar is dissolved and boiling starts.
3. Cook, stirring frequently, to 270°F on candy thermometer (soft-crack stage).
4. Pour on well-buttered marble slab or platter.
5. Fold outside edges into center of mixture as it cools to keep edges from becoming too brittle to pull.
6. When cool enough to handle, pull until lighter in color and texture.
7. Stretch into rope about ¾″ wide on buttered cookie sheet.
8. Cut in small pieces with scissors.
9. Wrap each piece in wax paper.
10. Store in tightly covered container.

## ORANGE TAFFY

1 cup sugar
¼ cup thawed frozen
  orange juice concentrate

1 tablespoon butter or
  margarine
few grains salt

1. In heavy 1-quart saucepan, mix all ingredients.
2. Cook over moderate heat, stirring continuously, to 262°F–264°F on candy thermometer (hard-ball stage).
3. Pour on buttered marble slab or platter.

4. Fold outside edges into center of mixture as it cools to keep edges from becoming too brittle to pull.
5. When cool enough to handle, pull until lighter in color and texture.
6. Stretch into rope about $\frac{3}{4}''$ wide on buttered cookie sheet.
7. Cut in small pieces with scissors.
8. Wrap each piece in wax paper.
9. Store in tightly covered container.

## Variation

FRESH LEMON TAFFY
1. Use 2 tablespoons fresh lemon juice and 2 tablespoons water in place of frozen orange juice concentrate in Orange Taffy.

## MELO-MINTS

2 cups sugar
$\frac{1}{4}$ cup butter
$\frac{2}{3}$ cup water

10 drops oil of peppermint or
1 teaspoon peppermint extract

1. In 2-quart saucepan, mix sugar, butter, and water.
2. Stir over moderate heat until sugar is dissolved and boiling starts.
3. Wipe down crystals from sides of pan with cloth wrapped around tines of fork dipped into hot water. Keep crystals wiped down during cooking. Continue to cook to 258°F on candy thermometer (hard-ball stage).
4. Pour on buttered marble slab.
5. Fold outside edges to center as candy cools to keep edges from becoming too brittle to pull.
6. When cool enough to handle, add flavoring and pull until mixture is light in color and texture.
7. Stretch into rope about $\frac{1}{2}''-\frac{3}{4}''$ thick on buttered slab or cookie sheet.
8. Cut in small pieces with scissors.

9. Let stand at room temperature until candy starts to "sugar" or become grainy. This may take several hours.
10. Put candy in tightly covered container. Let stand at least 1 day to become creamy.

Note: Mints may be colored and flavored as desired. Omit peppermint and use oil of any spice or lemon or orange, or use extracts of vanilla, lemon, or orange. Colorings may be added to candy while cooking or with the flavoring before pulling.

# BRITTLE, TOFFEE, AND CRUNCH

The texture of brittle, toffee, and crunch can almost be imagined by their names. For instance, can't you almost taste the rich crispness of peanut brittle as you say it?

A delicate addition to a candy assortment, these candies have only a few musts to remember in their preparation. Heavy pans should be used in cooking the candy sirup. They are needed to hold a more uniform heat during candy making.

Use the back of a buttered spoon for spreading any brittle candy.

When marking or cutting any firm or brittle candy, keep the blade of the knife or candy spatula clean by scraping it with the blade-edge of another knife.

Crunches should be kept boiling continuously to avoid separation of sugar and butter. If sugar and butter should separate, stir vigorously and cook rapidly until blended.

Heavy rubber gloves may be used when stretching hot brittles.

# PEANUT BRITTLE

2 cups sugar
1 cup light corn sirup
½ cup water
¼ teaspoon salt
2 cups raw Spanish
  peanuts

3 tablespoons butter or
  margarine
¼ teaspoon baking soda
½ teaspoon vanilla, if desired

1. In heavy 2-quart saucepan, mix sugar, corn sirup, water, and salt.
2. Stir over moderate heat until sugar is dissolved and boiling starts.
3. Cook, without stirring, to about 250°F on candy thermometer (firm-ball stage).
4. Add peanuts and butter or margarine.
5. Continue to cook over moderate heat, stirring continuously, to 295°F–300°F (hard-crack stage).
6. Remove from heat. Add baking soda which should be free from lumps and vanilla if used. Mix well, allowing mixture to foam a few seconds.
7. Pour on buttered marble slab or cookie sheet.
8. As soon as candy is firm enough on bottom to be picked up, which takes a few seconds on marble slab, loosen edges and bottom of brittle with spatula. Take hold of edges on one side and turn entire piece over.
9. Stretch and pull brittle as thin as desired. Turning and stretching are not necessary but give a thinner smoother peanut brittle.
10. When cold, break in pieces.
11. Store in tightly covered container.

## Variation
SALTED PEANUT BRITTLE
1. Cooking raw Spanish peanuts in brittle gives candy a rich flavor, but a very good peanut brittle may be made using salted peanuts. In this case, omit salt from Peanut Brittle.

10. Stretching peanut brittle

2. Cook candy to 285°F on candy thermometer (soft-crack stage). Then add salted Spanish peanuts and butter.
3. Continue cooking to 300°F (hard-crack stage).

## PECAN BRITTLE

| | |
|---|---|
| *1 cup small pecan nut-meats* | *⅛ teaspoon salt* |
| *1 cup sugar* | *2 tablespoons water* |
| *½ cup light corn sirup* | *2 tablespoons butter* |
| | *½ teaspoon vanilla* |

1. Warm nutmeats in 250°F oven for about 10 minutes.
2. In heavy 1-quart saucepan, combine sugar, corn sirup, salt, and water.
3. Cook, stirring occasionally, to 305°F on candy thermometer (hard-crack stage).

4. Add butter and vanilla. Stir over low heat until butter is blended.
5. Remove from heat. Add warm nutmeats, stirring in quickly.
6. Pour in buttered pan to depth of $\frac{1}{8}''$–$\frac{1}{4}''$.
7. Mark in squares when cool enough to hold markings and break apart when cold, or break into irregular-shaped pieces when cold.
8. Store in tightly covered container.

## Variation

COCONUT BRITTLE
1. Use 1 cup finely shredded coconut in place of the nutmeats in Pecan Brittle when candy is removed from heat.

## MIXED NUT BRITTLE

| | |
|---|---|
| 2 cups chopped, mixed nutmeats | $\frac{1}{4}$ teaspoon salt |
| 1$\frac{1}{2}$ cups sugar | 3 tablespoons butter or margarine |
| $\frac{3}{4}$ cup light corn sirup | $\frac{1}{2}$ teaspoon vanilla or |
| $\frac{1}{2}$ cup water | lemon extract, if desired |

1. Put nutmeats in 250°F oven to warm. If almonds are used, toast them first.
2. In heavy 2-quart saucepan, mix sugar, corn sirup, and water.
3. Stir over moderate heat until sugar is dissolved and boiling starts.
4. Cook, without stirring, to 305°F on candy thermometer (hard-crack stage).
5. Remove from heat. Add butter or margarine, salt, nutmeats, and flavoring if used, mixing quickly and thoroughly.
6. Pour in buttered pan to depth of $\frac{1}{4}''$.
7. Mark in squares or oblong pieces when candy sets or cool enough to hold markings. Break apart when cold.

8. Store in tightly covered container.

Note: A variety of nuts may be used, including cashews, black walnuts, brazil nuts, filberts, pecans, or toasted almonds.

## TOFFEE

¾ cup butter or
  margarine
1½ cups firmly packed,
  light brown sugar
¼ teaspoon salt
1 teaspoon vinegar
2 tablespoons water

½ pound milk chocolate or
  part milk chocolate and
  part dark sweet chocolate
1 cup finely chopped pecan
  nutmeats
½ teaspoon vanilla or rum
  extract, if desired

1. In heavy 2-quart saucepan, melt butter. Add sugar, salt, vinegar, and water.
2. Stir over moderate heat until sugar is dissolved and boiling starts.
3. Cook, stirring frequently, to 260°F on candy thermometer (hard-ball stage).
4. Cook over moderate heat, stirring continuously, to 295°F–300°F (hard-crack stage).
5. Remove from heat and add flavoring if used.
6. Pour in buttered pan to depth of about ⅛".

11. Pouring toffee

7. Spread warm melted chocolate on one side of hot toffee and cover thickly with pecans. Loosen candy and turn entire piece over. Coat second side with chocolate and nuts.
8. Let stand in cold room or refrigerator until chocolate is dry. Break in irregular-sized pieces.
9. Store in tightly covered container.

12. Spreading melted chocolate on toffee
13. Breaking toffee to store in tin box

# ALMOND CRUNCH

| | |
|---|---|
| *1 cup butter or margarine* | *¼ cup water* |
| *1½ cups sugar* | *¼ teaspoon salt* |
| *2 teaspoons light corn* | *1 cup blanched, coarsely chopped* |
| *  sirup* | *  or slivered toasted almonds* |

1. In heavy 2-quart saucepan or 8″ iron skillet, melt butter or margarine. Add sugar, corn sirup, water, and salt.
2. Stir until sugar is dissolved.
3. Cook, stirring occasionally, to 265°F on candy thermometer (hard-ball stage). Keep mixture boiling continuously over moderate heat.
4. Contine to cook, stirring gently and continuously, to 305°F (hard-crack stage).
5. Remove pan from heat. Add nuts and blend well.
6. Pour in lightly buttered pan to depth of about ¼″.
7. Mark in squares with heavy knife or candy spatula as soon as candy is cool enough to hold markings. Go over markings several times.
8. Break apart when cold. Dip in chocolate, if desired.
9. Store in tightly covered container.

## Variations

CASHEW CRUNCH
1. Use 1 cup toasted cashew nutmeats in place of almonds in Almond Crunch.

PECAN CRUNCH
1. Use 1 cup pecan nutmeats in place of almonds in Almond Crunch.

CHOCOLATE CRUNCH
1. Grind or crush Almond, Cashew, or Pecan Crunch in amount desired.
2. Mix with enough cooled melted milk chocolate to hold crunch together. Part milk chocolate and part dark-sweet chocolate may be used if desired.

3. Pour chocolate crunch mixture in wax-paper-lined pan to depth of $\frac{1}{2}''$.
4. Cut in squares when mixture starts to set and while chocolate is still soft enough to cut.
5. Store in tightly covered container.

## PEANUT CRUNCH

| | |
|---|---|
| $\frac{3}{4}$ cup butter or margarine | 3 tablespoons water |
| $1\frac{1}{2}$ cups sugar | $\frac{1}{8}$ teaspoon baking soda |
| 3 tablespoons light corn sirup | 2 cups finely chopped, roasted, salted peanuts |

1. In heavy 1-quart saucepan, melt butter. Add sugar, corn sirup, and water.
2. Stir over moderate heat until sugar is dissolved and boiling starts.
3. Cook, stirring occasionally, to 260°F–264°F on candy thermometer (hard-ball stage).
4. Continue to cook, stirring continuously, to 300°F (hard-crack stage).
5. Remove from heat. Add baking soda and mix well. Add peanuts and mix thoroughly.
6. Pour in buttered pan to depth of $\frac{1}{4}''$.
7. Mark in squares as soon as mixture will hold markings. Break apart when cold.
8. Store in tightly covered container.

## BUTTERSCOTCH CRISP

| | |
|---|---|
| 1 cup granulated sugar | $\frac{1}{4}$ cup water |
| $\frac{1}{2}$ cup firmly packed, light brown sugar | $\frac{1}{4}$ teaspoon salt |
| 1 teaspoon vinegar | $\frac{1}{2}$ cup butter |
| $\frac{1}{2}$ cup light corn sirup | $\frac{1}{2}$ teaspoon vanilla |

1. In 2-quart saucepan, combine sugars, vinegar, corn sirup, water, and salt.

2. Cook, stirring occasionally, to 260°F–265°F on candy thermometer (hard-ball stage).
3. Add butter. Continue to cook, stirring continuously, to 300°F (hard-crack stage). Add vanilla.
4. Pour in buttered pan to depth of $\frac{1}{8}$″–$\frac{1}{4}$″.
5. Mark in squares when cool enough to hold markings and break apart when cold, or break into irregular-shaped pieces when cold. Dip in chocolate, if desired.
6. Store in tightly covered container.

### Variation

Butterscotch Chews

1. Cook, without stirring, all ingredients in Butterscotch Crisp, except butter and vanilla, to 246°F on candy thermometer (firm-ball stage).
2. Add $\frac{1}{2}$ cup butter. Continue to cook, stirring occasionally, to 252°F–254°F (hard-ball stage). Add vanilla.
3. Pour in buttered pan to depth of $\frac{1}{2}$″.
4. When cold, cut and wrap in wax paper, or coat with chocolate.

## PEANUT BUTTER BRICKLE

*1 cup peanut butter*  
  *(creamy or chunky)*  
*1 cup sugar*

*$\frac{1}{3}$ cup light corn sirup*  
*$\frac{1}{3}$ cup water*

1. Place peanut butter over hot water to warm.
2. In 1-quart saucepan, combine sugar, corn sirup, and water.
3. Stir over moderate heat until sugar is dissolved.
4. Cook, without stirring, to 310°F on candy thermometer (hard-crack stage).
5. Pour immediately into peanut butter which has been removed from hot water. Blend thoroughly, working quickly.
6. Pour and pat in lightly buttered pan to depth of about $\frac{1}{2}$″.

7. Mark in squares immediately.
8. Break apart when cold.
9. Store in tightly covered container.

## Variation

Chocolate Peanut Butter Brickle
1. Grind or crush Peanut Butter Brickle in amount desired.
2. Mix with enough cooled melted milk chocolate to hold brickle together. Part milk chocolate and part dark sweet chocolate may be used if desired.
3. Pour chocolate brickle mixture in wax-paper-lined pan to depth of $\frac{1}{2}''$.
4. Cut in squares when mixture starts to set and while chocolate is still soft enough to cut.
5. Store in tightly covered continer.

## PEANUT BUTTER CRISP

| | |
|---|---|
| *1 cup sugar* | *1 teaspoon vinegar* |
| *$\frac{1}{3}$ cup light corn sirup* | *few grains salt* |
| *2 tablespoons light molasses* | *$\frac{1}{2}$ cup peanut butter* |

1. In 1-quart saucepan, mix sugar, corn sirup, molasses, vinegar, and salt.
2. Stir over moderate heat until sugar is dissolved and boiling starts.
3. Cook, stirring occasionally, to 300°F on candy thermometer (hard-crack stage).
4. Remove from heat. Add peanut butter and mix thoroughly.
5. Pour in buttered pan to depth of $\frac{1}{8}''$.
6. Mark in squares when mixture is cool enough to hold markings.
7. Break apart when cold.
8. Store in tightly covered container.

# COATED NUTMEATS

Nuts in a candy cookbook? Certainly, when they are covered with a sweet and interesting coating. Something about the crispness of the nutmeats and the smoothness of the candy cover makes them a favorite.

Since nutmeats are used in many candy recipes, here is a short course in different methods of dealing with them.

FRESHENING NUTMEATS
1. Any nutmeats, salted or unsalted, may be freshened by heating them in a moderate oven (350°F) for a few minutes.

BLANCHING NUTMEATS
1. Cover almonds and pistachio nutmeats with boiling water. Let stand several minutes or until skins loosen.
2. Drain off hot water. Rinse nuts in cold water.
3. Slip off skins with fingers or rub nuts between turkish towels.
4. Dry almonds in warm oven. Let pistachio nutmeats stand on paper towels to dry because oven heat may destroy their green color.

DRY TOASTING OR ROASTING NUTMEATS
1. Spread nutmeats in thin layer on cookie sheet.
2. Toast in preheated 250°F–300°F oven until light brown color. Stir frequently and watch closely. The time varies for different kinds of nutmeats. Pecans and walnuts take about 5–6 minutes. Filberts, cashews, and peanuts may take 20 minutes or more. Almonds take 40–60 minutes.

SALTING NUTMEATS

*1 cup vegetable oil*      *salt*
*nutmeats desired*

1. In heavy saucepan, heat vegetable oil to about smoking temperature (340°F–360°F).
2. Add $\frac{1}{2}$ cup nutmeats to the hot oil. Stir continuously until nuts are a light brown color. Nuts will darken slightly on cooling.
3. Remove with slotted spoon to paper towels or heavy brown paper.
4. While hot, sprinkle nuts generously with salt. Repeat process until all nutmeats are salted, adding more oil to pan if necessary.
5. When cold, store in tightly covered container.

## SPICED NUTMEATS

*$\frac{1}{3}$ cup sugar*      *$\frac{1}{8}$ teaspoon salt*
*1 teaspoon cinnamon*      *1 egg white*
*$\frac{1}{8}$ teaspoon ground cloves*      *1 cup nutmeats (pecans, walnuts,*
*$\frac{1}{8}$ teaspoon nutmeg*      *or toasted almonds)*

1. In small bowl, mix sugar, spices, and salt.
2. Beat egg white until soft peaks form. Add nutmeats a few at a time and coat thoroughly.
3. Drop egg-coated nutmeats in sugar and spice mixture. Use fingers to coat thoroughly.
4. Bake on ungreased cookie sheet in preheated 300°F oven for 20 minutes. Cool.

5. Store in tightly covered container.

## ORANGE CANDIED WALNUTS

*1 cup sugar*
*2 tablespoons thawed*
  *frozen orange juice*
  *concentrate*

*¼ cup water*
*2 cups walnut meats*
*⅛ teaspoon salt*

1. In saucepan, mix sugar, orange juice concentrate, and water.
2. Cook to 238°F on candy thermometer (soft-ball stage).
3. Remove mixture from heat. Add walnuts and salt. Stir until mixture is creamy.
4. Turn out on lightly greased pan or platter. Separate nuts with forks or fingers. Cool.
5. Store in tightly covered container.

## MINTED NUTMEATS

*1 cup sugar*
*3 tablespoons light corn*
  *sirup*
*¼ cup water*
*⅛ teaspoon salt*

*⅓ cup marshmallow creme*
*5–6 drops oil of peppermint*
  *coloring, if desired*
*2 cups walnut or pecan nutmeats*

1. In 1-quart saucepan, mix sugar, corn sirup, water, and salt.
2. Stir over moderate heat until sugar is dissolved and boiling starts.
3. Cook to 238°F on candy thermometer (soft-ball stage).
4. Remove from heat. Add marshmallow creme, peppermint, and coloring if used. Blend well.
5. Add nutmeats. Stir to thoroughly coat nutmeats.
6. Drop nuts on wax paper. Cool.
7. Store in tightly covered container.

## PENUCHE NUTMEATS

1 cup firmly packed, light
   brown sugar
3 tablespoons light corn
   sirup
¼ cup water

3 tablespoons butter or
   margarine
⅛ teaspoon salt
2 cups walnut or pecan nutmeats

1. In 1-quart saucepan, combine sugar, corn sirup, water, butter, and salt.
2. Stir over moderate heat until sugar is dissolved and boiling starts.
3. Cook, without stirring, to 238°F on candy thermometer (soft-ball stage).
4. Remove from heat. Add nutmeats and stir until mixture is creamy.
5. Turn out on lightly buttered pan and separate nutmeats. Cool.
6. Store in tightly covered container.

# A VARIETY OF CONFECTIONS

Many candies cannot be classified under specific headings, so this chapter is devoted to a variety of confections. Perhaps your favorite is among this sweet assortment.

## CANDIED ORANGE PEEL

*orange peels*  
*2 cups sugar*  
*1 cup light corn sirup*  
*1 cup water*

1. Remove peel from oranges in 4 lengthwise sections, or clean the remaining fiber from oranges used for juice, leaving white inner rind on.
2. Cover rind with cold water. Bring to boil slowly.
3. Remove from heat and drain well.
4. Repeat process 5 more times, so that rind is covered with cold water, brought to a boil, and drained 6 times in all. Rinse well each time. If rind does not seem tender after 5th cooking, let it simmer a few minutes until tender during the 6th and final cooking.
5. Make sirup of sugar, corn sirup, and water. Sirup should cover the amount of peel used.
6. Simmer peel and sirup mixture *very slowly* until peel is

clear and sirup is thick. This should take at least 3 hours. Stir mixture occasionally.

7. Let stand until cold. Remove pieces of peel from sirup and drain well.
8. Cut in strips to roll in granulated sugar, or dip in chocolate. Candied peel keeps for months in the refrigerator.

## Variation

CANDIED GRAPEFRUIT OR LEMON PEEL

1. Use grapefruit or lemon peel or a combination of peels in place of the orange peel in Candied Orange Peel.

## CANDIED FRUIT

| | |
|---|---|
| 2 cups sugar | 2 teaspoons lemon juice |
| 1 cup light corn sirup | fruit desired (dried prunes, |
| ½ cup water | apricots, peaches, raisins, figs) |

1. In 2-quart saucepan, combine sugar, corn sirup, water, and lemon juice.
2. Stir over moderate heat until sugar is dissolved and boiling starts.
3. Boil about 2 minutes to 240°F on candy thermometer (soft-ball stage).
4. Add 8–10 pieces of fruit at one time. Dried fruit may be steamed a few minutes before being candied if a softer texture is desired.
5. Simmer very slowly, stirring carefully, 6–8 minutes. Lift fruit from sirup with slotted spoon into strainer to drain 5–10 minutes.
6. Remove to lightly buttered cookie sheet and let stand several hours to dry.
7. Repeat candying process until all fruit desired is candied.
8. Roll in granulated or confectioners' sugar.
9. Store in tightly covered container. Use within a few days.

## QUICK MINTS

1 cup sugar
3 tablespoons light corn
  sirup
¼ cup water

¼ cup marshmallow creme
coloring, if desired
4 drops oil of peppermint

1. In 1-quart saucepan, mix sugar, corn sirup, and water.
2. Stir over moderate heat until sugar is dissolved and boiling starts.
3. Cook, without stirring, to 238°F on candy thermometer (soft-ball stage).
4. Remove from heat. Add marshmallow creme and coloring if used.
5. Stir until mixture begins to lose its gloss (5–10 minutes).
6. Add peppermint, blending thoroughly.
7. Turn out on wax paper.
8. When cool, wrap in wax paper. Keep tightly covered to ripen at least 1 hour.
9. Mold into desired shapes. Dip in chocolate. For mint

14. Making quick mints

patties, melt ripened mixture in small pan or double boiler over hot, not boiling, water, stirring gently. Drop from teaspoon in small patties on wax paper.

10. Keep in tightly covered container. Mint mixture may be kept in lump for several days but will soften slightly on standing.

## CHOCOLATE CREME FUDGE

| | |
|---|---|
| 2 1-ounce squares unsweetened chocolate | $\frac{1}{4}$ cup milk |
| 3 tablespoons butter or margarine | 3 tablespoons light corn sirup |
| | $\frac{1}{4}$ cup marshmallow creme |
| 1 cup sugar | $\frac{1}{2}$ teaspoon vanilla |
| $\frac{1}{4}$ teaspoon salt | $\frac{1}{3}$ cup chopped nutmeats, if desired |

1. In 1-quart saucepan, melt chocolate and butter or margarine over low heat. Stir continuously.
2. Add sugar, salt, milk, and corn sirup.
3. Stir over moderate heat until sugar is dissolved and boiling starts.
4. Cook, stirring occasionally, to 236°F on candy thermometer (soft-ball stage).
5. Remove from heat. Add marshmallow creme.
6. Stir until mixture begins to lose its gloss (5–10 minutes).
7. Add vanilla and nutmeats if used. Blend thoroughly.
8. Pour in wax-paper-lined pan. Cut when set.
9. Store in tightly covered container.

### Variation

PEANUT BUTTER FUDGE

1. Omit chocolate in Chocolate Creme Fudge.
2. Add $\frac{1}{4}$ cup smooth or chunky peanut butter with vanilla.

# CHOCOLATE-MALO FUDGE

| | |
|---|---|
| 12 ounces semi-sweet chocolate | 3 tablespoons corn sirup |
| 2 cups firmly packed, chopped marshmallows | $\frac{1}{8}$ teaspoon salt |
| 3 tablespoons milk | $\frac{1}{2}$ teaspoon vanilla |
| | $\frac{1}{2}$ cup chopped nutmeats, if desired |

1. Melt chocolate over hot water, stirring frequently. Semi-sweet chocolate pieces or bits may be used if desired.
2. In saucepan, combine marshmallows, milk, corn sirup, and salt.
3. Stir over very low heat or over hot water until marshmallows are melted. Add vanilla.
4. Combine chocolate and marshmallow mixture. Blend thoroughly. Add nutmeats if used, stirring in well.
5. Pour in wax-paper-lined pan.
6. When firm, cut as fudge, or shape in balls and roll in chopped nutmeats, coconut, or chocolate sprinkles, or shape for centers to be dipped in chocolate.

## EASY FRUIT FUDGE

| | |
|---|---|
| 2 tablespoons butter or margarine | $\frac{1}{4}$ teaspoon glycerin |
| 2 cups sifted confectioners' sugar | $\frac{1}{8}$ teaspoon salt |

Any of the following:

   2 tablespoons thawed frozen orange juice concentrate
   2 tablespoons thawed frozen grape juice concentrate
   2 tablespoons thawed frozen pineapple juice concentrate

1. Melt butter or margarine. Add remaining ingredients.
2. Mix until thoroughly blended.
3. Pat in wax-paper-lined pan to depth of $\frac{1}{2}''$.
4. For fudge, cut. For chocolate dipping, wrap in wax paper and let ripen for 1–2 days. Then mold into desired shapes and dip in chocolate.

# UNCOOKED FUDGE

2 tablespoons butter or
   margarine
1 tablespoon light corn
   sirup or honey

$\frac{1}{4}$ teaspoon salt
$1\frac{1}{2}$ teaspoons vanilla
$1\frac{1}{2}$ cups sifted confectioners'
   sugar

1. Melt butter or margarine. Add remaining ingredients. Blend thoroughly. If mixture is too soft, add more confectioners' sugar. If mixture is too stiff, add few drops milk or water.
2. Pat out in wax-paper-lined pan and allow to ripen 1–2 days in refrigerator. Cut for fudge, or roll in balls to dip in cooled melted chocolate.
3. Store in tightly covered container.

## Variations

CHOCOLATE FUDGE
1. Melt 1–2 ounces unsweetened chocolate with butter in Uncooked Fudge.

COCONUT FUDGE
1. Add $\frac{1}{2}$ cup shredded coconut when adding other ingredients to butter in Uncooked Fudge.

NUT FUDGE
1. Add $\frac{1}{2}$ cup finely chopped nutmeats or $\frac{1}{4}$ cup peanut butter when adding other ingredients to butter in Uncooked Fudge.

# CREAM CHEESE FUDGE

1 3-ounce package cream
   cheese
2 teaspoons melted butter
   or margarine
2 teaspoons light corn
   sirup
$\frac{1}{8}$ teaspoon salt

$2\frac{1}{2}$ cups sifted confectioners' sugar
2 1-ounce squares melted
   unsweetened chocolate
$\frac{1}{2}$ teaspoon vanilla
$\frac{1}{2}$ cup chopped nutmeats

1. Soften and cream the cheese.
2. Add melted butter, corn sirup, and salt. Mix thoroughly.
3. Slowly stir sugar into creamed mixture.
4. Add melted chocolate, vanilla, and nutmeats. Blend well.
5. Press into wax-paper-lined pan. Chill until firm. Cut into squares.
6. Store tightly covered in refrigerator.

## NUT BARK

small pecan halves or
toasted almonds

milk chocolate or
half milk chocolate and half
dark sweet chocolate

1. Line 8"-square pan with wax paper. Cover with layer of nuts.
2. Melt chocolate over hot, not boiling, water to have about 1 cup melted chocolate. Cool to dipping temperature (84°F–90°F).
3. Pour chocolate in thin coat over nuts.
4. Mark in squares when chocolate begins to set but while it is still soft, or let mixture cool and break in irregular-shaped pieces.

## KRINGLE BARK

peppermint stick candy

milk chocolate or
half milk chocolate and half
dark sweet chocolate

1. Grind peppermint stick candy in desired amount into small mixing bowl.
2. Melt chocolate to have about same amount as stick candy. Cool to dipping temperature (84°F–90°F).
3. Pour chocolate over peppermint candy and mix in quickly.
4. Pour in wax-paper-lined pan to depth of $\frac{1}{8}$".

5. Mark in squares when chocolate begins to set but while it is still soft, or let mixture cool and break into irregular-shaped pieces.

## CHOCOLATE COCONUT STACKS

*milk chocolate*  *shredded coconut*
*semi-sweet chocolate*

1. Melt equal parts milk chocolate and semi-sweet chocolate over hot water.
2. Cool chocolate to dipping temperature (84°F–90°F).
3. Mix shredded coconut with melted combined chocolate in equal proportions.
4. Drop with teaspoon or fingers in "piles" on wax paper.
5. When cold, store in tightly covered container.

## COCONUT BONBONS

$\frac{1}{3}$ *cup sugar*  *3 cups finely shredded coconut*
$\frac{3}{4}$ *cup light corn sirup*  *1 teaspoon vanilla*
$\frac{1}{4}$ *teaspoon salt*

1. In 1-quart saucepan, cook sugar, corn sirup, and salt to 228°F on candy thermometer. For firmer bonbon, cook to 236°F (soft-ball stage).
2. Remove from heat. Add coconut and vanilla and mix thoroughly. Leave in pan to cool.
3. When cool, roll in small balls. If mixture is too sticky to roll, mix in more coconut.
4. Dip in melted fondant or chocolate.

### Variations

COCONUT-PECAN BONBONS
1. Add $\frac{1}{4}$ cup finely chopped nutmeats with coconut and vanilla in Coconut Bonbons.

CANDIED FRUIT BONBONS

1. Add ¼ cup finely chopped candied cherries or other candied fruit with coconut and vanilla in Coconut Bonbons.

15. Bonbon dipping

## FRENCH CHOCOLATES

12 ounces milk chocolate or
   dark sweet chocolate
3 tablespoons corn sirup
3 tablespoons evaporated
   milk

⅛ teaspoon salt
½ cup chopped nutmeats, if
   desired

1. Melt chocolate over hot water, stirring continuously. Semi-sweet chocolate pieces or bits may be used if desired.
2. Remove from heat. Add corn sirup, milk, and salt. Blend thoroughly. Add nutmeats if used.
3. Pour in wax-paper-lined pan to depth of $\frac{1}{2}''$.
4. When firm, cut as for fudge, or shape in balls and roll in chopped nutmeats, coconut, or chocolate sprinkles.

## Variation

FRENCH MINTS
1. Omit nutmeats from French Chocolates.
2. Add $\frac{1}{4}$ teaspoon oil of peppermint with corn sirup, milk, and salt in French Chocolates.
3. Cut as for fudge, then dip in chocolate.

# MARSHMALLOW CREME

*1 cup sugar*
*⅔ cup light corn sirup*
*⅛ teaspoon salt*

*1 egg white*
*1 teaspoon vanilla*

1. In 1-quart saucepan, mix sugar, corn sirup, and salt.
2. Stir over moderate heat until sugar is dissolved and boiling starts.
3. While sirup cooks, beat egg white until stiff peaks form.
4. Cook sirup, without stirring, to 236°F on candy thermometer (soft-ball stage).
5. Pour cooked sirup slowly into egg white, beating continuously with electric or hand beater until mixture is very thick. Add vanilla and mix thoroughly.
6. Pour in covered container and store in refrigerator.
7. May be used in all candy recipes calling for marshmallow creme. May also be used in cake frosting recipes.

# CHOCOLATE CLUSTERS

*1 cup cooled, melted dark-sweet chocolate or milk chocolate*
Any of the following:
*1 cup nutmeats desired or combination of salted or unsalted nutmeats*
*1 cup seedless or seeded raisins or combination of candied fruit cut in small pieces and mixed together*
*1 cup any kind ready-to-eat cereal or combination of cereals*

1. In 1-quart bowl or pan, combine nutmeats, fruit, or cereal and 1 cup cooled melted chocolate.
2. Mix thoroughly and drop on wax paper with teaspoon or fingers. If chocolate hardens before all clusters are dropped, remelt chocolate very slightly over hot water, stirring continuously.
3. When dry, store tightly covered in cool place.

## BASIC PRALINES

*1 cup firmly packed, light brown sugar*
*1 cup granulated sugar*
*2 tablespoons butter or margarine*
*1 teaspoon vinegar*
*¼ teaspoon salt*
*1 cup 18% cream*
*1 cup coarsely broken pecan nutmeats*
*½ teaspoon vanilla*

1. In 2-quart saucepan, mix sugars, butter or margarine, vinegar, and salt. Add cream.
2. Stir over moderate heat until sugar is dissolved and boiling starts.
3. Cook to 236°F on candy thermometer.
4. Remove from heat. Let cool to about 150°F.
5. Beat until mixture starts to lose its gloss, then add pecans and vanilla.
6. Pour quickly to about ¼″ in buttered muffin tins, or drop from teaspoon onto wax paper.
7. Remove when cold. Wrap in wax paper.
8. Store in tightly covered container.

## Variations

CREAMY PRALINES

1. Start beating Basic Pralines at a cooler temperature of about 110°F (lukewarm).

CHEWY PRALINES

1. Add ½ cup light corn sirup to other Basic Praline ingredients in saucepan.
2. Cook to 240°F–242°F on candy thermometer (firm-ball stage).
3. Remove from heat. Add nutmeats and vanilla. Mix thoroughly.
4. Pour in buttered muffin tins.
5. When cold, wrap each praline in wax paper.
6. Store in tightly covered container.

### POPCORN BALLS

| | |
|---|---|
| *6–8 cups popped corn* | *3 tablespoons butter or* |
| *1 cup sugar* | *margarine* |
| *⅓ cup light or dark corn* | *1 teaspoon vanilla* |
| *sirup* | *½ teaspoon salt* |
| *¼ cup water* | |

1. Have corn popped and measured in buttered pan or bowl.
2. In heavy 1-quart saucepan, cook sugar, corn sirup, and water to 295°F–300°F on candy thermometer (hard-crack stage).
3. Remove from heat. Add butter or margarine, vanilla, and salt. Mix well.
4. Pour over popcorn. With 2 forks, mix quickly until kernels are well coated.
5. Roll mixture into balls when cool enough to handle. Rinse hands with water or coat with butter if mixture is too sticky to handle.
6. When balls are cold, wrap in wax paper, twisting the ends.

## Variations

OLD-FASHIONED MOLASSES POPCORN BALLS AND CARAMEL CORN

1. Omit vanilla from Popcorn Balls.
2. Add 2 tablespoons molasses to work with other Popcorn Ball ingredients in saucepan.
3. For Molasses Popcorn Balls: follow directions in Popcorn Balls.
4. For Caramel Corn: spread mixture on buttered cookie sheet. When cold, break apart in clusters.

NUT POPCORN BALLS AND CARAMEL CORN

1. Replace some of the popcorn in Old-Fashioned Molasses Popcorn Balls with roasted peanuts or a combination of pecan halves and toasted almonds.
2. For Nut Popcorn Balls: follow direction in Popcorn Balls.
3. For Nut Caramel Corn: spread mixture on buttered cookie sheet. When cold, break apart in clusters.

CEREAL CRISPS

1. Use 6–8 cups dry cereal (1 kind or several kinds mixed together) in place of popcorn in Popcorn Balls.

## SCOTCHIES

| | |
|---|---|
| $\frac{1}{4}$ cup butter | $\frac{1}{3}$ cup light corn sirup |
| 1 cup firmly packed, light brown sugar | $\frac{1}{8}$ teaspoon salt |
| | $\frac{1}{4}$ cup evaporated milk |

1. In heavy 1-quart saucepan, melt butter.
2. Add sugar, corn sirup, and salt.
3. Cook, stirring, to 250°F on candy thermometer (hard-ball stage).
4. Add evaporated milk. Continue to cook, stirring frequently, to 244°F–246°F (firm-ball stage).
5. Pour in buttered pan to depth of $\frac{1}{2}''$.
6. When cold, cut in small squares.

7. Wrap in wax paper, or dip in chocolate.

**Variation**

HEAVENLY HASH

1. Make 1 recipe Scotchies and let stand in pan to cool to about 175°F on candy thermometer.
2. Add 1 cup miniature marshmallows and ½ cup coarsely chopped walnuts or pecans. Add ¼ cup chocolate bits or ¼ cup shredded coconut with marshmallows and nutmeats if desired.
3. Blend well and pour in buttered pan to depth of about ½″.
4. Let stand overnight to become firm. Cut as for fudge.
5. Store in tightly covered container.

## HARD CANDY
## (SQUARES, BALLS, AND LOLLIPOPS)

| | |
|---|---|
| *1 cup sugar* | *2 tablespoons water* |
| *½ cup light corn sirup* | *few grains salt* |
| *¼ teaspoon cream of tartar* | *coloring desired* |

Any of the following:

| *Flavoring Oils* | *Flavoring Extracts* |
|---|---|
| *½ teaspoon cinnamon* | *2 teaspoons vanilla* |
| *½ teaspoon orange* | *2 tablespoons raspberry* |
| *½ teaspoon clove* | *2 teaspoons cherry* |
| *½ teaspoon lemon* | *2 teaspoons orange* |

1. In heavy 1-quart saucepan, combine all ingredients except flavoring and coloring.
2. Stir over moderate heat until sugar is dissolved and boiling starts.
3. Cook, stirring occasionally, to 300°F on candy thermometer (hard-crack stage).
4. Remove from heat. Add flavoring, oils or extracts, and coloring.

5. For squares: Pour in buttered pan to depth of about ½″. Mark in squares when cool enough to hold markings. Break apart when cold.
6. For Balls: Pour small amount of mixture on marble slab which has been lightly buttered and thickly coated with granulated sugar. Keep remaining mixture in pan over low heat. Cut candy on slab with knife or scissors and quickly roll into balls. Roll in sugar. Repeat until all mixture is used.
7. For Lollipops: Drop from teaspoon on buttered marble slab. Press one end of round toothpick or skewer into edge. Loosen candy from slab as soon as firm to avoid cracking when cold. When cold, wrap in wax paper.
8. Store hard candy in tightly covered container in cool place.

### STUFFED DATES

*pitted dates*
*fondant, walnuts, or
toasted almonds*

*granulated sugar, or
shredded coconut, or
cooled melted chocolate*

1. Stuff pitted dates with fondant, walnuts, or toasted almonds.
2. Roll in granulated sugar or finely shredded coconut, or dip in cooled melted chocolate.

### PENUCHE NIBLETS

*2 cups firmly packed, light
brown sugar*
*¼ cup butter or margarine*
*½ cup light corn sirup*

*½ cup evaporated milk*
*¼ teaspoon salt*
*¾ cup coarsely chopped walnut or
pecan meats*

1. In heavy 2-quart saucepan, combine all ingredients except nutmeats.
2. Stir over moderate heat until boiling starts.
3. Cook over moderate heat, stirring frequently, to 238°F on candy thermometer (soft-ball stage).

4. Remove from heat and stir mixture until thick enough to hold its shape.
5. Add nutmeats.
6. Drop from teaspoon on wax paper, or mixture may be poured in wax-paper-lined pan and cut as fudge.

## FRUIT BALLS

| | |
|---|---|
| $\frac{1}{2}$ cup pitted dates | $\frac{1}{2}$ cup walnut meats |
| $\frac{1}{2}$ cup raisins | $\frac{1}{3}$ cup finely shredded |
| 8 dried figs | coconut |
| $\frac{1}{4}$ cup candied cherries | $\frac{1}{4}$ teaspoon salt |
| $\frac{1}{4}$ cup candied pineapple | $\frac{1}{4}$ cup orange juice |

1. Put fruits, nuts, and coconut through coarse blade of food chopper.
2. Add salt and orange juice. Mix thoroughly.
3. Roll in balls. If mixture is too moist, add confectioners' sugar.
4. Roll balls in finely ground nutmeats, shredded coconut, or confectioners' sugar.
5. Store tightly covered.

## CHOCOLATE ACORNS

| | |
|---|---|
| blanched, lightly toasted almonds | ground nutmeats or colored sprinkles |
| cooled melted chocolate | |

1. Dip large end of whole almonds in chocolate.
2. Dip coated end in ground nutmeats or colored sprinkles. Let dry.
3. Store in tightly covered container.

## COLORED SUGAR

| | |
|---|---|
| 1 cup granulated sugar | 4–6 drops desired food coloring |

1. Blend sugar and food coloring. Stir or mix with fingers to blend thoroughly.

2. Store tightly covered.

## COLORED COCONUT

*1 cup finely shredded*          *4–6 drops desired food coloring*
  *coconut*

1. Blend coconut and food coloring. Stir or mix with
   fingers to blend thoroughly.
2. Store tightly covered.

## ROYAL ICING FOR CANDY
## DECORATING

*2 egg whites*                    *few grains salt*
*1 teaspoon lemon juice*          *3 cups confectioners' sugar*
*⅛ teaspoon cream of*             *½ teaspoon glycerin*
  *tartar*                        *coloring, if desired*

1. Add lemon juice, cream of tartar, and salt to egg
   whites.
2. Beat until blended and foamy.
3. Gradually add sugar, beating until so stiff that will not
   drop from a spoon. Add glycerin and coloring if used
   during last part of beating.
4. Since icing becomes crusty, cover immediately after
   preparing.
5. Use Royal Icing in a pastry bag to decorate Easter
   eggs, lollipops, mint patties, etc.
6. If icing becomes too thick, add small amount of water.
   If icing becomes too thin, add more confectioners'
   sugar.
7. To keep, cover tightly.

## MOLDING CHOCOLATE

1. Buy molds desired from a variety of shapes and sizes
   available in confectioner supply houses.

2. Be sure molds are dry and at dipping-room temperature (60°F–68°F). Do not put molds in refrigerator.
3. Fill molds with cooled melted chocolate (dark sweet or milk chocolate).
4. Let stand in cold room for 1 hour or more to dry.
5. Remove chocolate shapes from molds using wax paper or foil to handle so heat and moisture from hands does not mar gloss of chocolate.
6. Store tightly covered in cool place.

# CHOCOLATE DIPPING

Chocolate dipping is perhaps the most creative part of candy making, but it is also the most exacting. Certain rules must be followed if the dipping is to be successful. So read this chapter, then read it again; and after several study sessions, practice. Knowledge coupled with practice will have you producing dipped candy worthy of a professional.

Chocolate, the most usual coating for dipped centers, is made from the cocoa bean. Many varieties of cocoa beans are grown, and many blends are created to make various grades of chocolate. The better qualities give the best gloss and flavor.

## KINDS OF CHOCOLATE COATINGS

DARK SWEET CHOCOLATE (Semi-Sweet Chocolate)

This chocolate is used for almost all candy to be dipped. It comes in 10-pound cakes and is sold in baker supply stores and chocolate manufacturing companies, and in some candy stores where candy is made. Also sold in $\frac{1}{2}$-pound amounts and in pieces (called semi-sweet chocolate bits or morsels) in grocery stores.

### BITTERSWEET CHOCOLATE

This chocolate is used to cover very sweet centers. It comes in 10-pound cakes and is sold in baker supply stores and chocolate manufacturing companies, and in some candy stores where candy is made.

### MILK CHOCOLATE

This chocolate makes a slightly heavier coating to work with in dipping. It can be thinned by adding 1 tablespoon melted cocoa butter (available in drug stores) to 1 pound milk chocolate. It comes in 10-pound cakes and is sold in baker supply stores and chocolate manufacturing companies, and in some candy stores where candy is made. Also sold in large broken pieces and bars in the candy section of many stores.

## CENTERS SUITABLE FOR DIPPING

1. Creamed candy
2. All firm and brittle candies
3. Jellies and marshmallows
4. Dried or candied fruit, candied fruit peels, and nut-meats.

## GENERAL DIPPING INFORMATION

1. Approximately $\frac{1}{2}$ pound of chocolate will cover 1 pound of centers to be dipped.
2. The room in which chocolate dipping is done should have optimum dipping conditions. The chocolate may dry when dipping conditions are unfavorable, but it will not have the glossy appearance which chocolate should have.
3. Melting of chocolate in preparation for dipping should be done without subjecting the chocolate to extreme heat. Overheating detracts from its gloss and flavor.
4. Chocolate coating too cool for dipping makes the piece of candy too heavy and rough in appearance.
5. Never allow water to get into chocolate at any time, because water thickens chocolate.

6. Do not cover chocolate while melting or while warm after it has been melted. Steam may condense on the lid, and water will drop into the chocolate.

7. Shaped centers ready for dipping should not be colder than room temperature. If centers are too cold, the chocolate chills too quickly and will not dry with a gloss.

8. Your hands should be normal in temperature. If they are too warm, some chocolate is overheated as it leaves your hands, and the chocolate dries leaving gray streaks. If your hands are too cold, chocolate hardens on them.

9. Leftover melted chocolate should be poured in a wax-paper-lined pan and stored for future use. Chocolate can be remelted and used.

10. Store all unused chocolate coating in a cool place. Wrap it thoroughly or store it in a metal box. Due to the facts that cocoa butter does not change or deteriorate easily and that chocolate has a low moisture content, chocolate keeps for months. Milk chocolate is more perishable than dark sweet or bittersweet, so it is best always to store it in a metal container.

11. The gray streaks on chocolate may appear at any time during the making and storing of chocolates when proper care is not observed in the control of heat and humidity. This does not necessarily affect the flavor of the chocolate, except in extreme cases when chocolate has been overheated. The grayish streaks (called "bloom" by professional candy makers) may be caused either by improper mixing and cooling (called "tempering") of chocolate in preparation for dipping or by too much humidity in the air.

12. Platforms on the bottom of the chocolate-dipped candy may be caused by too much chocolate left on the piece of candy as it is dropped on the paper, pressure put on the piece of candy as it is dipped and dropped, or by the chocolate's being too warm so that it does not dry fast enough.

# PREPARATION FOR CHOCOLATE DIPPING

1. The room in which chocolate dipping is done should: be free from steam and strong drafts; have a temperature of 60°F–68°F; have a humidity below 55%.
2. Assemble all materials and equipment used for dipping.
3. About 1 hour before candy is ready to be dipped, break the chocolate into small pieces on a wooden board, using an ice pick.

16. Breaking chocolate to melt in double boiler

4. Melt the chocolate slowly, uncovered, in the top part of a double boiler over hot, not boiling, water. Stir the chocolate frequently as it melts. It is best not to have the temperature of the melted dark sweet or bittersweet chocolate higher than 120°F on the candy thermometer. The water in the lower part of the double boiler should be 150°F–175°F. Milk chocolate should be melted more

slowly than dark chocolate and stirred continuously as it melts. The temperature of milk chocolate should not go higher than 115°F.

5. Cover the table used for dipping with disposable papers for easier clean-up.
6. Cover trays or lightweight boards with wax paper to hold the dipped candy.
7. Use any small pan to hold the melted chocolate while dipping. A lightweight metal skillet or pie or cake tin about 8″ wide and 2″ deep is convenient.
8. Have the centers ready for dipping.

## PREPARING CENTERS FOR DIPPING

CREAMED CANDY

1. Roll creamed candy into a rope about ½″ in diameter.
2. Cut the rope into pieces about ¾″ long.
3. Roll pieces lightly between the palms of your hands into the desired shapes such as balls, small ovals, larger ovals for Easter eggs, etc. Use a small amount of cornstarch on your hands if candy is sticky.
4. Place the pieces on wax paper. A light coating of cornstarch may be used on the wax paper to keep the candy from sticking to the paper if necessary.
5. Let the creamed candy stand about 30 minutes until

17. Molding creamed candy for chocolate coating

a light crust forms before dipping. This makes the candy easier to handle during the dipping process.

FIRM AND BRITTLE CANDIES

1. Cut the candy into squares or oblong pieces.

JELLIES AND MARSHMALLOWS

1. Cut the candy into squares or oblong pieces. Shape Easter eggs with scissors.
2. Brush off all excess sugar.

DRIED OR CANDIED FRUIT, CANDIED FRUIT PEELS, AND NUTMEATS

1. Cut dried or candied fruit into small pieces. Cut fruit peels in strips. Do not roll them in sugar before dipping. Nutmeats may be lightly toasted and cooled, salted or unsalted.

## DIPPING PROCEDURE

1. Put a portion of the melted chocolate in the dipping pan. Use 1 pound or more to maintain the proper dipping temperature longer.
2. Add several cold lumps of chocolate and work them into the warm chocolate with the fingers until the mixture feels cool to the touch. For dark sweet or bittersweet chocolate, the proper dipping temperature is 84°F–90°F on the candy thermometer. For milk chocolate, the proper dipping temperature is about 82°F.
3. Put the lumps of chocolate aside or back in the double boiler to melt.
4. With the tray of centers which are to be dipped on the left of the dipping pan, pick up one center with your left hand and put it in the chocolate.
5. With your right hand, roll and cover the piece with chocolate. Pick it up with your right thumb and middle finger. Turn your palm up, manipulating the piece of

candy until it is resting on the tip of your middle finger supported by your thumb.

6. Brush the back of your hand lightly across the rim of the pan to remove excess chocolate. Turn your palm down, over the wax-paper-covered tray to the right. Let the chocolate-dipped piece drop from your finger, with the aid of your thumb if necessary.

18. Coating candy with chocolate

7. Move your thumb and middle finger across and above the piece of candy so that the string of melted chocolate dripping from them forms a design on the top of the candy. Try these designs after a little experience in dipping.

8. Let the piece stay where it falls. Do not touch or move it until it is dry.

9. After dipping 6–8 pieces, check the first dipped candy to see if it is beginning to dry. If not, check again on the temperature of the room and the temperature of the

chocolate. The chocolate should dry in a few minutes. If not, it dries without a gloss or with gray streaks.

10. Add any decorations such as nutmeats, colored sprinkles, etc. to the chocolate-dipped piece before the chocolate dries. Any chocolate-coated additions may be added after the chocolate piece is dry.

11. When the chocolate in the dipping pan gets too cold and heavy to continue dipping, warm the pan slowly over hot water, or add more hot melted chocolate and cool again to dipping temperature with more cold lumps of chocolate.

12. After the coating has dried, with a little chocolate on the tips of your fingers, touch up the places on the piece of chocolate which have leaked. Leaks may be due to improper covering which leaves thin places that allow the center to break through as it "works" or softens inside the coating.

13. If a large amount of chocolate dipping is to be done, add more lumps of chocolate to the double boiler to melt as you work.

14. To dip with a fork or bonbon dipper, drop the piece to be coated in melted cooled chocolate (84°F–90°F or 82° depending on what kind of chocolate you are

19. Dipping candy in chocolate with fork

using). With the fork, cover the piece with chocolate. Balancing the piece on the fork, lift out the piece and tap the fork on the rim of the pan. Draw the fork carefully across the rim to remove excess chocolate. Invert the fork and let the chocolate-dipped piece drop onto the wax-paper-covered tray.

## CARE OF CHOCOLATE-DIPPED CANDY

1. Let the tray of dipped chocolates stand at dipping-room temperature until the candies are thoroughly dry (at least 30 minutes) before removing them from the paper.
2. Remove the chocolates carefully from the wax paper. Pick them up lightly from the sides and release them quickly so that the heat and moisture from your hands does not destroy the gloss of the chocolate.
3. Store the chocolates covered and in a wax-paper-lined box with wax paper between the layers. Store at about 65°F or cooler. Maintain as even a temperature as possible for best keeping.
4. Allow the chocolates to stand several days to "mellow" before using.

## LIGHT COATING FOR DIPPING (WHITE CHOCOLATE)

Light coating, which is sometimes called white chocolate, is a vegetable fat compound using mainly the fats of vegetables instead of cocoa butter. The coating is available in white and pastel colors and may be purchased from the same sources as chocolate. This coating is easy to work with in dipping. It may be used at slightly warmer temperatures, and the temperature and humidity of the room may be slightly higher than for chocolate dipping. The care of candy in light coating is the same as that of centers dipped in chocolate.

# PREPARATION OF LIGHT COATING
## FOR DIPPING

1. Break light coating in small lumps on a wooden board.
2. Melt it over hot, not boiling, water. The temperature of the light coating should not go higher than 115°F on the candy thermometer, and the water in the bottom of the double boiler should be 150°F–175°F. Stir continuously while melting because light coating melts easily and quickly. Be very careful not to overheat, for this thickens the coating.
3. Put a portion of the melted coating in the dipping pan. Add several cold lumps of coating and work them into the warm coating with your fingers until the mixture feels cool to the touch (88°F–95°F). Light coating in the dipping pan may need more frequent remelting than chocolate does to keep it at dipping consistency.
4. Any candy center desired may be dipped in light coating. The stronger-flavored centers such as chocolates, mints, tart jellies, and fruit mixtures are especially good.
5. Dip centers as you would in chocolate.

## PACKING CANDY

1. The box to hold the candy may be lined with special liners or wax paper cut to size.
2. Place one end of the box on top of the upside-down lid so that the box slants. The angle allows the box to be filled completely with the candy's slipping and sliding less.
3. Gather the assortment desired on a tray placed to the left of the box to hold the candy.
4. Hold the paper candy cup in your left hand. Quickly place the dipped candy in the paper cup. Remember to hold the dipped candy lightly on the sides so the glossy finish is not marred.
5. Place the candy in paper cups into the box.

20. Packing candy in boxes

6. The spaces in the box may be filled in with chocolate-covered nutmeats or coated hard candies which do not require the protection of paper cups.
7. To add to the shine of chocolate, brush the top of the candy lightly with a camel's hair brush.
8. Now the box is ready for its final wrapping. If the boxes are to be kept, store them in a cool place or freeze them to retain the freshness (directions on p. 13).

# ESPECIALLY FOR CHILDREN

Let's call this section "Especially for Children," for perhaps this is where the children can get into the act. What better way to acquaint them with the intricacies and fun of cooking than with candy—which uses simple ingredients, easy cooking procedures, and elementary equipment, and yet produces sweet results in a short time. Here are assembled several easy-to-prepare candies. You'll find other recipes in the book which boys and girls should have fun preparing too.

## UNCOOKED FONDANT

2 tablespoons butter or
   margarine
1 tablespoon light corn
   sirup

¼ teaspoon salt
1 teaspoon vanilla
1½ cups sifted confectioners'
   sugar

1. Melt butter or margarine. Add remaining ingredients.
2. Blend thoroughly. If mixture is too soft, add more confectioners' sugar. If mixture is too stiff, add few drops milk or water.
3. Pat out in wax-paper-lined pan. Cut for fudge if desired.

4. Store tightly covered.
5. For molding fondant, wrap candy in a lump in wax paper until ready to use for molding. If candy is not to be used for a few days, store in plastic bag in refrigerator. When ready to mold, if candy is too stiff, add few drops of milk or water. If candy is too moist, add more confectioners' sugar.

**Variation**

ARTISTS' PARTY FONDANT
1. Make supply of Uncooked Fondant to use for "modeling."
2. Have a variety of food coloring and some small paint brushes.
3. Mold fondant on cookie sheets, using confectioners' sugar on hands and cookie sheets if fondant is sticky. Start by molding and coloring fondant in the easier shapes such as strawberries, pumpkins, bananas, carrots, etc. The party may end with people making many kinds of original figures, even caricatures ready-to-eat for the party desert.

## CHOCOLATE DROPS

| | |
|---|---|
| *1 tablespoon butter or margarine* | *⅛ teaspoon salt* |
| | *1 cup sweetened condensed milk* |
| *2 cups semi-sweet chocolate bits* | *½ cup chopped nutmeats or finely shredded coconut or seedless raisins, if desired* |
| *1 tablespoon light corn sirup* | *1 teaspoon vanilla* |

1. In top part of double boiler, melt butter or margarine and chocolate bits. Stir with wooden spoon.
2. Add corn sirup, salt, and condensed milk. Mix well.
3. Cook, stirring frequently, about 15 minutes. Keep water boiling in bottom part of double boiler.
4. Remove from heat.

5. Add nutmeats, coconut, or raisins if used and vanilla. Stir to mix well.
6. With a teaspoon, drop candy in small mounds on buttered cookie sheet.
7. When cold, store covered.
8. For covered chocolate balls, when Chocolate Drops are cool enough to handle, roll each piece in ground nutmeats, finely shredded coconut, or colored sprinkels.

## REFRIGERATOR FUDGE

2 1-ounce squares
 semi-sweet chocolate
2 tablespoons butter or
 margarine
½ cup sweetened con-
 densed milk
⅛ teaspoon salt

1 tablespoon light corn sirup
1⅓ cups non-fat dry milk
 powder
1 teaspoon vanilla
½ cup finely chopped nutmeats, or
 finely shredded coconut, or
 seedless raisins, if desired

1. In 1-quart saucepan, melt chocolate and butter or margarine. Stir with wooden spoon as it melts.
2. Remove from heat. Add all remaining ingredients. Stir until thoroughly mixed.
3. Pat out in square on wax paper. Put in refrigerator to harden. Cut in pieces.
4. Store tightly covered.

## SIX-MINUTE FUDGE

¼ cup butter or margarine
⅓ cup evaporated milk
¼ cup light corn sirup
⅛ teaspoon salt
1 cup sugar

1 cup firmly packed, chopped or
 miniature marshmallows
1 cup semi-sweet chocolate bits
1 teaspoon vanilla
½ cup chopped nutmeats

1. In heavy 1-quart saucepan, melt butter or margarine.
2. Add evaporated milk, corn sirup, salt, and sugar.
3. With wooden spoon, stir over medium heat until mixture is boiling.

4. Keep mixture boiling over medium heat, stirring around bottom and sides of pan to keep candy from scorching. Boil 6 minutes. Start counting on clock when candy begins to boil with bubbles covering entire surface of candy (a rolling boil).
5. Remove from heat. Add marshmallows and chocolate. Stir until melted.
6. Add vanilla and nutmeats. Mix well.
7. Pour in wax-paper-lined pan. Cut when firm.
8. Store tightly covered.

## MARSHMALLOW CEREAL CRISPS

$\frac{1}{4}$ cup butter or margarine
2 cups firmly packed, chopped or miniature marshmallows

$\frac{1}{8}$ teaspoon salt
2 cups ready-to-eat cereal
$\frac{1}{2}$ teaspoon vanilla

1. In top part of double boiler, melt butter and marshmallows. Stir while melting.
2. Remove from heat. Add salt, cereal, and vanilla. Mix well to coat cereal.
3. Quickly drop small clusters from tip of teaspoon onto buttered cookie sheet, or mixture may be poured in one piece and cut when firm.

Note: $\frac{1}{4}$ cup chopped nutmeats, or $\frac{1}{2}$ cup shredded coconut, or $\frac{1}{4}$ cup peanut butter may be added with the cereal.

### Variations

CHOCOLATE CEREAL CRISPS
1. Melt 1 1-ounce square semi-sweet chocolate with butter or margarine and marshmallows in Cereal Crisps.

POPCORN CRISPS
1. Use 2 cups popped corn in place of the cereal in Cereal Crisps.

# MAKING CANDY
# IN QUANTITY

Remember the sentence in the introduction, the one refer-
ring to candy making's being a profitable business as well
as an interesting and rewarding hobby? Let's talk about
making candy in quantity, something which is excellent for
gift-giving and money-making for your favorite charity.
Some of the assets are the fun and sociability that come from
working with good food and learning something together
with an enthusiastic group.

To work efficiently and make candy in quantity easily,
let's organize.

## ORGANIZATION FOR MAKING CANDY
## IN QUANTITY

PLANNING AHEAD
1. Decide the kinds and amounts of candy to be made.
2. Plan the work schedule.
3. Check the equipment needed according to the recipes
   used (see "Equipment for Candy Making," page 7–8).
4. Figure out the kinds and amounts of supplies needed
   and decide where to buy.

5. If you are going to sell the candy, decide where to sell, how to sell, and the prices to charge.

ORGANIZE WORKING GROUPS

1. General Manager: To be responsible alone or with selected helpers for buying supplies, setting up and carrying out general working plans and procedures, and then checking progress.
2. Cookers
3. Molders
4. Chocolate dippers
5. General helpers
6. Packers

WORKING PROCEDURE

1. With the necessary supplies on hand, the cookers start a few days earlier than the other workers. All firm and brittle candy can be made in advance and kept in tightly covered containers, until time for chocolate dipping.
2. The molders shape the creamed centers, putting pieces on wax-paper-lined trays ready for chocolate coating. They cut firm candy (caramels, chews, jellies, etc.) and place the pieces on wax-paper-lined trays for chocolate coating, or wrap the pieces in wax paper.
3. The chocolate dippers are responsible for complete care of the chocolate. They melt the chocolate in preparation for coating. Then, taking the trays of centers from the molders, they coat the pieces with chocolate and place them on wax-paper-lined trays.
4. The helpers are valuable workers, lending a hand wherever needed. In the chocolate-coating department, they move the coated candy from the dipping trays to wax-paper-lined storage boxes. These boxes should hold only 4 or 5 layers of candy per box, with wax paper between each layer. Each piece of candy

may be put in a paper candy cup before being put in the storage container.

5. The packers pack the finished candy in wax-paper-lined boxes. They then wrap the containers for selling.

SUGGESTED CANDY TO SELL FOR FUND-RAISING

1. Assorted chocolates. Pack in candy boxes which are wrapped and ready for selling.
2. Various fudges cut in squares. Pack in wax-paper-lined box and cover tightly.
3. Caramels. Wrap each piece in wax paper or cellophane and pack in boxes with tight covers.
4. Caramel Corn and Popcorn Crisp. Pack in small and/or large air-tight plastic or cellophane bags.
5. Melo-Mints, in various colors and flavors. Pack in tightly covered tin boxes or glass jars.
6. Peanut Brittle. Pack in air-tight plastic or cellophane bags or in tightly covered tin boxes.

Following are selected popular recipes which should sell well. Remember, however, that all the candy recipes in the book may be enlarged to suit your situation.

## BASIC VANILLA CREAMS (QUANTITY)

6 cups sugar
3 cups 18% cream
$\frac{1}{3}$ cup light corn sirup
$\frac{3}{4}$ teaspoon salt

1 tablespoon vanilla
$1\frac{1}{2}$ cups chopped nutmeats,
 if desired

1. In 6-quart saucepan, mix sugar, cream, corn sirup, and salt.
2. Stir over moderate heat until sugar is dissolved and boiling starts.
3. Cook, without stirring, to 236°F on candy thermometer (soft-ball stage).
4. Pour on lightly buttered marble slab.
5. Cool to lukewarm or cooler.

6. Add vanilla and work with candy spatulas until firm enough to handle. Add nutmeats if used.
7. Knead until creamy. Do not overknead—just a few strokes may be enough.
8. Wrap in wax paper and keep tightly covered until ready to use for chocolate-dipped centers.

Recipe yield: approximately 3½ pounds.

## BASIC CHOCOLATE FUDGE
## (QUANTITY)

*6 cups sugar*
*3 cups 18% cream*
*¾ teaspoon salt*
*⅓ cup light corn sirup*

*6 1-ounce squares melted unsweetened chocolate*
*1½ teaspoons vanilla*

1. In 6-quart saucepan, mix sugar, cream, salt, and corn sirup.
2. Stir over moderate heat until sugar is dissolved and boiling starts.
3. Cook, without stirring, to 336°F on candy thermometer (soft-ball stage).
4. Pour on buttered marble slab.
5. Pour melted chocolate over candy. Do not stir.
6. When lukewarm, add vanilla.
7. Work with candy spatulas until creamy. Knead a few strokes.
8. Pat out in wax-paper-lined pan to depth of ½″. Cut when firm.

Recipe yield: approximately 4 pounds.

### Variation

CREAMS TO BE DIPPED IN CHOCOLATE
1. Cook Basic Chocolate Fudge to 234°F on candy thermometer (soft-ball stage).
2. Cool to lukewarm. Add vanilla and 2 teaspoons glycerin.

3. Work until firm enough to handle. Knead until creamy.
4. Wrap in wax paper and store tightly covered until ready to be molded into shapes.

## PEANUT BRITTLE (QUANTITY)

*3 cups sugar*
*1½ cups light corn
   sirup*
*¾ cup water*
*½ teaspoon salt*

*2½–3 cups raw Spanish
   peanuts*
*¼ cup butter or margarine*
*½ teaspoon baking soda*
*1 teaspoon vanilla, if desired*

1. In heavy 3-quart saucepan, mix sugar, corn sirup, water, and salt.
2. Stir over moderate heat until sugar is dissolved and boiling starts.
3. Cook, without stirring, to about 244°F on candy thermometer (firm-ball stage).
4. Add peanuts and butter or margarine.
5. Continue to cook over moderate heat, stirring continuously, to 300°F (hard-crack stage).
6. Remove from heat. Add baking soda which should be free from lumps and vanilla if used.
7. Pour on buttered marble slab or 2 large cookie sheets.
8. As soon as candy is firm enough on bottom to be picked up (this takes just a few seconds on marble slab), loosen edges and bottom of brittle with spatula. Take hold of edges on one side and turn entire piece over.
9. Stretch and pull as thin as desired.
10. When cold, break in pieces.
11. Store tightly covered.

Recipe yield: approximately 3 pounds

## PENUCHE (QUANTITY)

*3 cups firmly packed, light
   brown sugar*

*2 tablespoons light corn sirup*
*¾ teaspoon salt*

| | |
|---|---|
| 3 cups granulated sugar | 2 cups chopped nutmeats, if |
| 3 cups 18% cream | desired |

1. In 6-quart saucepan, mix all ingredients except nut-meats.
2. Stir over moderate heat until sugar is dissolved and boiling starts.
3. Cook, without stirring, to 236°F on candy thermometer (soft-ball stage).
4. Pour on buttered marble slab.
5. Cool to lukewarm and work until creamy. Add nut-meats if used.
6. Pour or pat out in wax-paper-lined pan to depth of $\frac{1}{2}''$.
7. For fudge, cut when firm. For centers to be dipped in chocolate, keep in tightly covered container until ready to be molded into shapes.

Recipe yield: approximately 3 pounds

## CARAMELS (QUANTITY)

| | |
|---|---|
| 4 cups sugar | 3 cups 18% cream |
| 2⅔ cups light corn sirup | ¾ cup evaporated milk |
| 1 teaspoon salt | 2 teaspoons vanilla, if desired |
| ¼ pound butter or margarine | 2 cups chopped nutmeats, if desired |

1. In heavy 6-quart saucepan, mix sugar, corn sirup, salt, butter or margarine, and 1½ cups of the cream.
2. Stir over moderate heat until sugar is dissolved and boiling starts.
3. Cook, stirring frequently, to 238°F–240°F on candy thermometer.
4. Add remaining 1½ cups of the cream and cook again to 238°F–240°F, stirring frequently.
5. Slowly add evaporated milk, pouring in thin stream

and stirring continuously so that mixture continues to boil.

6. Continue to cook, stirring continuously, to 240°F–242°F for a soft caramel or 244°F–246°F for a firm caramel.
7. Remove from heat. Let stand about 5 minutes.
8. Stir in vanilla and nuts if used and pour in buttered pan to depth of about ½″.
9. Let cool at least several hours. Turn out on wooden board or marble slab. If caramel sticks to pan in which it has been cooled, hold pan a few inches above a low heat for a few minutes to release caramel. Cut in small squares using a sawing motion.
10. Wrap in wax paper, or dip in chocolate.
11. Store in tightly covered container in cool place.

Recipe yield: approximately 4 pounds

## BASIC POPCORN CRISP (QUANTITY)

| | |
|---|---|
| *12–14 cups popped corn* | *⅓ cup butter or margarine* |
| *2 cups sugar* | *2 teaspoons vanilla* |
| *⅔ cup light corn sirup* | *1 teaspoon salt* |
| *½ cup water* | *coloring, if desired* |

1. Have corn popped and measured in large buttered pan or bowl.
2. In heavy 2-quart saucepan, cook sugar, corn sirup, and water to 295°F–300°F on candy thermometer (hard-crack stage).
3. Remove from heat. Add butter or margarine, vanilla, salt, and coloring if used. Mix well.
4. Pour over popcorn. Mix quickly until kernels are well coated.
5. When cold, break apart in clusters.
6. Store tightly covered.

Recipe yield: approximately 2½ pounds

**Variations**

NUT POPCORN CRISP
1. Use roasted peanuts, pecans, toasted almonds, or a combination of any nutmeats desired in place of some of the popped corn in Basic Popcorn Crisp.

CARAMEL POPCORN CRISP
1. Add $\frac{1}{4}$ cup molasses in saucepan to cook with ingredients for Basic Popcorn Crisp.

## ALMOND CRUNCH (QUANTITY)

| | |
|---|---|
| *1 pound butter or margarine* | *$\frac{1}{3}$ cup water* |
| *3 cups sugar* | *$\frac{1}{2}$ teaspoon salt* |
| *1 tablespoon light corn sirup* | *2 cups coarsely chopped or slivered toasted almonds* |

1. In heavy 3-quart saucepan, melt butter or margarine.
2. Add sugar, corn sirup, water, and salt.
3. Stir until sugar is dissolved, then stir occasionally to 265°F on candy thermometer (hard-ball stage). Keep mixture boiling continuously over moderate heat.
4. Cook, stirring continuously, to 305°F (hard-crack stage).
5. Remove from heat. Add nuts and blend well.
6. Pour in lightly buttered pan to depth of about $\frac{1}{4}''$, or pour on unbuttered marble slab.
7. If candy is poured in pan, mark in squares with heavy knife or candy spatula as soon as candy is cool enough to hold markings. Go over markings several times. Break apart when cold. If candy is poured on marble slab, cut in $\frac{1}{2}''$ strips, then in pieces. Work quickly because crunch hardens rapidly. Helpers are necessary.
8. Dip crunch in chocolate, if desired.
9. Store in tightly covered container.

Recipe yield: approximately $2\frac{1}{2}$ pounds

## BASIC ORIENTALS (QUANTITY)

| | |
|---|---|
| 6 *cups sugar* | 2 *teaspoons glycerin* |
| 2 *cups water* | ¼ *teaspoon salt* |
| ⅓ *cup light corn sirup* | 2 *medium egg whites* |
| ⅛ *teaspoon cream of* | *flavoring desired* |
| *tartar* | *coloring, if desired* |

1. In 2-quart saucepan, mix sugar, water, corn sirup, cream of tartar, glycerin, and salt.
2. Stir over moderate heat until sugar is dissolved and boiling starts.
3. Cover pan and let boil 2–3 minutes.
4. Uncover pan. Wipe down sugar crystals from sides of pan with cloth wrapped around tines of fork which has been dipped in hot water. Wipe down crystals several times during cooking.
5. Cook, without stirring, to 240°F–242°F on candy thermometer (soft-ball stage).
6. Pour on cold damp marble slab.
7. Cool to lukewarm.
8. Add stiffly beaten egg whites, flavoring, and coloring if used.
9. Work with candy spatulas until creamy. This takes much longer than for other creamed candies and for a while may not appear to be creaming.
10. Let stand 10–15 minutes to set. Mold into desired shapes for chocolate coating. A small amount of cornstarch may be used on hands to make molding easier. If pieces of candy seem soft, place on wax paper which has been lightly dusted with cornstarch.
11. When thin crust has formed on shaped pieces, which takes about 20–30 minutes, dip in chocolate.

Recipe yield: approximately 3 pounds

### Variations

PEPPERMINT ORIENTALS

1. Add $\frac{1}{2}$ teaspoon oil of peppermint when starting to work Basic Orientals.

#### WINTERGREEN ORIENTALS
1. Add $\frac{1}{2}$ teaspoon oil of wintergreen and a few drops of red coloring (to make mixture pink) when starting to work Basic Orientals.

#### VANILLA ORIENTALS
1. Add 1 tablespoon vanilla when starting to work Basic Orientals.

#### COCONUT ORIENTALS
1. Add 1 tablespoon vanilla and 2–3 cups finely shredded coconut near the end of creaming Basic Orientals.

#### PECAN ORIENTALS
1. Add 1 tablespoon vanilla and 2 cups finely chopped pecan nutmeats near the end of creaming Basic Orientals.

# INDEX